UKRAINE

Series on Religion, Nationalism, and Intolerance

UKRAINE
The Legacy of Intolerance

David Little, *Director*

Working Group on Religion, Ideology, and Peace

UNITED STATES
INSTITUTE OF PEACE PRESS

Washington, D.C.

274.77
L77u

United States Institute of Peace
1550 M Street, N.W.
Washington, D.C. 20005

First published 1991

Printed in the United States of America

Library of Congress Cataloging-in-Publication Data
Little, David, 1933-
    Ukraine : the legacy of intolerance / David Little.
    p. cm. — (Series on religion, nationalism, and intolerance)
    ISBN 1-878379-12-7
    1. Ukraine—Church history—20th century. 2. Nationalism—Ukraine—
History—20th century. 3. Nationalism—Religious aspects—Christianity.
I. Title. II. Series.
BR937.U4L57 1991
274.7'71082—dc20   91-20695
TP   CIP

United States Institute of Peace

The United States Institute of Peace is an independent, nonpartisan, federal institution created and funded by Congress to strengthen the nation's capacity to promote the peaceful resolution of international conflict. Established in 1984, the Institute has its origins in the tradition of American statesmanship, which seeks to limit international violence and to achieve a just peace based on freedom and human dignity. The Institute meets its congressional mandate to expand available knowledge about ways to achieve a more peaceful world through an array of programs including grantmaking, a three-tiered fellowship program, research and studies projects, development of library resources, and a variety of citizen education activities. The Institute is governed by a bipartisan, fifteen-member Board of Directors, including four members ex officio from the executive branch of the federal government and eleven individuals appointed from outside federal service by the President of the United States and confirmed by the Senate.

Contents

Foreword

The breathtaking changes that have occurred in Eastern Europe and, to a lesser extent, in the Soviet Union over the past two years have brought substantially greater political and economic freedom to these areas. But Mikhail Gorbachev's policies of glasnost and perestroika have produced some unanticipated—and unfortunate—consequences as well. The removal of old restrictions that kept deep-seated religious and nationalist antagonisms in check has allowed those antagonisms to assert themselves vigorously.

Ukraine, for example, has recently been the locus of serious religious conflict. The present hostilities primarily involve three churches of the Eastern Byzantine tradition: the Ukrainian Catholic church (also called Greek-Catholic or Uniate), the Ukrainian Autocephalous Orthodox church, and the Russian Orthodox church. The national churches—especially the Catholics and the Autocephalous Orthodox—were severely suppressed and their clergy persecuted beginning in the 1920s and 1930s. In particular, Catholic and Autocephalous churches and other religious buildings were confiscated and transferred to the Russian Orthodox as part of Stalin's policy of using the Russian Orthodox church as a means of ''Russifying'' areas like Ukraine. The Russian Orthodox church administered these buildings in close cooperation with the Soviet government until 1987 or so, when Gorbachev began to institute his reforms.

With the liberalization of the policy on religion, Catholics and Autocephalous Orthodox wanted their confiscated property back. However, the Russian Orthodox hierarchy were not inclined to comply. They have never been keen to recognize the legitimacy of the national churches and frequently have described them as nationalist political fronts rather than authentically religious bodies.

This conflict, focusing originally on the dispute over church property, has led to the recent "strife of the churches" in Ukraine. And now the national churches themselves are at odds with each other. Ukrainian Catholics and Autocephalous Orthodox are engaged in their own bitter and potentially violent disputes, sometimes involving the use of church property in western Ukraine. Some members of each side challenge the national loyalty of the other side.

For many reasons, then—including the historical character of religion in this area, the Marxist legacy, and the predilections of Russian Orthodoxy—religion and nationalism are inextricably intertwined. Beliefs about national independence for Ukraine are closely tied to deeply held convictions in favor of liberty of conscience and the right to practice religion free of Russian domination and interference by the Soviet central government. Freedom of religion is seen to depend on freedom of national identity. Whether such beliefs are, finally, "really" religious or "really" nationalist in character appears to be unanswerable.

Moreover, the conflict in Ukraine is fueled by irreconcilable accounts of historical grievances. Each party has its story to tell. Not only are the various stories of how things got to where they are different, at points, they are mutually incriminating. They justify one side and accuse the other. Disagreements over the historical accuracy of opposing accounts are deep and intense. The prospects for modifying some of these antagonistic accounts—these conflicting beliefs—are not altogether encouraging at present.

On the other hand, unless some common story, some inclusive and shared account of past and present, can be reconstructed out

of the diverse and mutually hostile interpretations that character-
ize the current struggle in Ukraine, the chances for lasting and just
peace in that land are not strong.

There are, as a matter of fact, some promising developments. Both
in the Soviet government and, perhaps more important, in the
Ukrainian national movement that is increasingly attempting to take
charge of Ukrainian destiny, efforts at constitutional revision to
guarantee religious pluralism and liberty of conscience are already
underway.

Indeed, on one level, the Ukrainian case presents a ringing
endorsement of the cause of religious pluralism and liberty of belief.
The seventy-year campaign of religious discrimination and persecution perpetrated by the Soviet government was, by all accounts,
a complete failure. It is now widely and passionately affirmed
throughout Ukraine that only a genuine system of religious pluralism and freedom of conscience has a chance of overcoming the legacy of intolerance and the tradition of violence bequeathed for so long
to the Ukrainian people.

Certain fundamental alterations have been called for, some of
which are beginning to take place. Change is already apparent in
the behavior of both the Russian Orthodox church and the Soviet
central government regarding the monopoly over religious life they
have historically enjoyed, although the present situation is obviously
fluid. Perhaps most important of all, at this point, further alterations are still required to reduce the antagonism between the national churches over who most authentically represents the new
spirit of Ukrainian nationalism (as the information provided in the
afterword makes particularly vivid).

Ukraine: The Legacy of Intolerance is the first report in a six-part
study of belief and intolerance sponsored by the United States Institute of Peace. This study is a project of the Institute Working
Group on Religion, Ideology, and Peace, which was established
to consider (1) how religious and similar beliefs sometimes

contribute to conflict as well as (2) methods for managing such conflict and encouraging peaceful pluralism.

   As the basis for the study, the working group will conduct six two-
day conferences over a period of two years. The group has already
taken up Ukraine, Sri Lanka, and Lebanon; in 1991 and 1992 it will
consider Sudan and Nigeria (together), Tibet, and Israel. The cases
have been chosen to exemplify different cultural and belief traditions, various geographical and political settings, and diverse types
of intolerance. Some of the cases—particularly Sri Lanka, Lebanon,
the Sudan, Nigeria, and Israel—are of special interest because at
one time or another they have been committed to pluralistic arrangements. All the cases illustrate the ways in which the modern
imperatives of nationalism set the context for much of the religious
and ideological conflict currently taking place. By focusing on these
important examples, the working group should be able to draw
some useful conclusions about the causes of this kind of conflict
as well as the prospects for peaceful resolution.

                              Samuel W. Lewis, President
                          United States Institute of Peace

About the Series

This six-part study of belief and intolerance considers how and why certain religious and similar beliefs create or contribute to hostility and conflict, as well as how and why they are frequently a cause of discrimination and persecution. In addition, it addresses the prospects and techniques for modifying and ameliorating conflicts that involve religious and similar loyalties and commitments. It asks how stable arrangements of mutual respect and forbearance come about. What are the resources, both inside and outside traditions of belief, that encourage ''peaceful pluralism'' and thereby prevent differences in basic outlook from leading to mistreatment, abuse, and violence?

Such an investigation is squarely within the mandate of the United States Institute of Peace. The Institute is an independent, nonpartisan government institution created and funded by Congress to strengthen the nation's capacity to promote the peaceful resolution of international conflict (or conflict with serious international implications). The Institute pursues its mandate by awarding grants, by appointing scholars and practitioners as fellows, by producing publications and educational programs, and by assembling working groups to share ideas and conduct research.

The study is the project of the Institute Working Group on Religion, Ideology, and Peace. By directing the attention of twenty or so experts to the subject of belief and intolerance, we expect to draw some useful conclusions regarding one aspect, at least, of the causes of serious conflict and the means of resolving it.

The context for this reflection will be six two-day conferences spread over a period of roughly two years. Each conference is devoted to an area of the world where serious intercommunal tension or conflict exists and where intolerance based on religion or belief appears to be a significant part of the difficulty. The working group has already taken up Ukraine (June 1990), Sri Lanka (September 1990), and Lebanon (November 1990). In 1991 it will consider the Sudan and Nigeria (in combination), Tibet, and Israel. Reports on each of these conferences, written by the director of the working group, David Little, will follow in due course.

The inspiration for the study is the momentous set of concerns enunciated in the UN Declaration on the Elimination of All Forms of Intolerance and of Discrimination Based on Religion or Belief, adopted by the UN General Assembly in November 1981. In view of the fact, states the preamble, ''that the disregard and infringement of human rights and fundamental freedoms of thought, conscience, religion or whatever belief, have brought. . .wars and great suffering to mankind,'' the General Assembly declares itself to be ''convinced that freedom of religion and belief should. . .contribute to the attainment of the goals of world peace, social justice and friendship among peoples. . . .''

Widespread violation of religious liberty and freedom of conscience make such a study urgent. According to current information compiled by the UN special rapporteur on intolerance and discrimination, ''infringement of the rights defined in the Declaration against Intolerance seem to persist in most regions of the world. . . . They concern all the provisions of the Declaration.''[1]

The Special Rapporteur is concerned with the persistence of alarming infringements of other human rights arising out of attacks on freedom of thought, conscience, religion or belief. Noteworthy among them is the growing number of extra-judicial killings that have allegedly taken place in the context of clashes between religious groups or between such groups and security forces. Resorting to violence or the threat of its use in dealing with problems or antagonisms of a religious nature is also a disturbing development which, if unchecked, might endanger international peace.[2]

The most important factors hampering the implementation of the Declaration are: the existence of legal provisions that run counter to the spirit and letter of the Declaration; practices by governmental authorities, contradicting not only the principles embodied in international instruments but even provisions enshrined in domestic law which prohibit discrimination on religious grounds; the persistence of political, economic and cultural factors which result from complex historical processes and which are at the basis of current expressions of religious intolerance (p. 56).

In some instances, a state's constitution extends special privileges by conferring official status on one religious or ideological group. In others, special legislation favors one or more religions to the detriment of excluded groups, and in extreme examples, certain religions or denominations are declared to be unlawful and members are punished for belonging to those groups or practicing their tenets (p. 11).

Beyond legislative provisions, government practices and policies frequently violate the terms of the declaration by encouraging disparagement of specific groups by means of the state-controlled media, educational policy, or denying in practice any legal status or legal protection to the members of a religion not recognized officially. Governments sometimes tolerate and even encourage abuses perpetrated by one group against another, or directly interfere in the practices and activities of certain religious bodies (pp. 11–12).

Finally, political, economic, and cultural factors frequently breed distrust and bigotry.

Norms, judgments, prejudices, superstitions, myths, and archetypes whereby we model our behavior in society and which are culturally transmitted from generation to generation, as well as anachronistic and unjust economic structures that result in regional majorities of human beings sunk into misery and ignorance, all foster the germination of dogmatism, intolerance, and discrimination, and with it persecution and armed aggression. These norms, judgments and prejudices, which give rise to deep feelings and to the transformation of unfocused emotions into sharp feelings that condition our ideas about equality among human beings, as well as tolerance and respect for the ideas and feelings of others, are a product of societal forces. This means that in order to eliminate discrimination and intolerance in all their forms there must necessarily be a change in attitude of the human being which will be a product of the needed social changes and psychic transformations of individuals.[3]

The declaration is clear that all forms of basic belief, and not just religious belief, are explicitly protected. People may not be punished or discriminated against, regardless of whether their basic beliefs are religious.[4]

However, the declaration is not altogether clear or consistent about the exact meaning of intolerance.[5] At one point, intolerance is synonymous, and used interchangeably, with discrimination (see Appendix, article 2.2). To discriminate, according to the declaration, is to impose a restriction or preference "based on religion or belief" that denies basic human rights and freedoms, such as freedom of expression, freedom of worship, equal access to public facilities, and so on. It is presumed, incidentally, that the declaration also prohibits persecution, or the direct infliction of severe injury or distress, as simply an extreme form of discrimination.

At another point, however, the declaration suggests that intolerance and discrimination are different things. The title itself speaks of "the Elimination of All Forms of Intolerance *and* of Discrimination'' (emphasis added). What is more, states are obligated under the declaration to prohibit discrimination legislatively, but they are urged ''to take all appropriate measures to combat intolerance'' (see Appendix, article 4.2), as though they were dealing with distinct phenomena.

Perhaps the proper interpretation is that, strictly speaking, intolerance refers to motives and attitudes, whereas discrimination refers to acts. Accordingly, ''intolerance describes the emotional, psychological, philosophical and religious attitudes that may prompt acts of discrimination. . . .''[6] This formulation raises the related question whether the outward expression of intolerant attitudes—such as taunting, insulting, or inflaming people because of belief—while not constituting actual discrimination as such, is still prohibited under the declaration insofar as it may be shown to incite discrimination. Such a proposition, of course, poses standard perplexities concerning the proper limits of free speech.[7]

Bearing the proposed distinction between intolerance and discrimination in mind, it will, in this study, nevertheless be convenient (and not altogether inconsistent with the declaration or with ordinary usage) to use the word *intolerance* occasionally in a less refined and more inclusive way to cover acts of discrimination (and persecution) as well as motives and attitudes that incite to such action. In that sense, *intolerance based on religion or belief* may at times refer to abusive practices as well as to the feelings and dispositions behind those practices.[8]

It is important to emphasize the specific and rather elaborate sense in which the word *intolerance* is used in the declaration to counteract the lingering suspicion that the very notions of tolerance and intolerance are outmoded and need to be replaced. The word *tolerance* recalls, it is said, arrangements in which a majority merely indulges certain unconventional beliefs as a matter of sufferance, not of right. On that basis, adherents are hardly given equal respect or treated without discrimination. According to this older notion, those unwilling to bear with such an indulgent system would be called intolerant. But under contemporary conditions, the idea of intolerance appears to convey considerably more than that.[9]

However accurate this observation may be historically, the concept of intolerance as specified in the declaration prohibits all arrangements that rest on or produce attitudes or conditions of serious discrimination or the inferiorization of certain groups because of religion or belief. By implication, the idea of tolerance would exclude any such attitudes and conditions.

A central objective of the project, then, is to test carefully and thoughtfully the twofold proposition that intolerance, as described, contributes substantially to wars and great suffering and that its modification or elimination helps to promote justice, solidarity, and peace.

Approach

The comparative study of intolerance and belief, such as is described here, has not been taken up elsewhere. It represents, it is hoped, a distinctive complement to related work in regard to nation building, communal conflict, and human rights.

The study is not envisioned as a rigorous social-scientific exercise replete with quantified results aimed at verifying some comprehensive theory of intolerance. The subject matter is so complex and varies so from place to place that it appears at this stage to defy any such aspiration. A more exploratory, informal, and open-ended approach seems preferable.

Moreover, whatever explanatory account is finally adopted for why people believe as they do and what they make of their beliefs, there is no substitute for first determining carefully what those beliefs are and how believers themselves understand, defend, apply, and are disposed to alter their beliefs. Unless that job is done well, explanatory accounts will be deficient. In short, the study takes seriously the subjective meaning of belief as expressed by participants and informed observers of the areas to be examined.

It should also be said that—for working purposes, at least—a *belief* shall be understood as a state of mind disposed to regard a proposition or set of propositions as true. *Belief that* something is true seems to be a necessary condition for holding a belief, however expanded the idea may become when people talk, as they often do in discussions of religious and ideological matters, of *believing in* someone or something. The kind of special trust, confidence, or commitment usually associated with basic or fundamental beliefs of a religious or related sort seems to presuppose that those beliefs are taken to be true in the first place.[10]

This emphasis on belief does not mean that the investigation is indifferent to material factors, such as the motive to protect or achieve sheer economic or political advantage for one's group. These factors are sometimes understood to be external to the core doctrines of the respective belief traditions and to condition in various ways the connections between belief and intolerance. Part of the task of the study will be to detect and trace those connections, at least informally and suggestively, insofar as they exist.

Such a task is, of course, notoriously complicated, because basic religious and other beliefs so readily become entangled with questions of ethnic, economic, and national identity and competition. On the one hand, religious or other basic beliefs are occasionally manipulated in the service of political or economic interests. Machiavelli's famous advice to princes comes to mind:

It is well to seem merciful, faithful, humane, sincere, religious, and also to be so; but you must have the mind so disposed that when it is needful to be otherwise you may be able to change to the opposite qualities. . . . A prince must take great care that nothing goes out his mouth which is not full of the above. . .qualities, and, to see and hear him, he should seem to be all mercy, faith, integrity, humanity, and religion. . . . [N]othing is more necessary than to seem to have this last quality. . . . Everybody sees what you appear to be, few feel what you are. . . . A certain prince. . .never does anything but preach peace and good faith, but he is really a great enemy to both, and either of them, had he observed them, would have lost him state or reputation on many occasions.[11]

On the other hand, religion or similar beliefs typically play an active and prominent part in defining group identity and in picking out and legitimating particular ethnic and national objectives. For example, political and economic competition among groups is frequently couched in religious terms, and attitudes toward members of other groups and ways of treating them are themselves understood religiously.

Max Weber reminds us of "the need of social strata, privileged through existing political, social, and economic orders, to have their social and economic positions 'legitimized.'" Groups "wish to see their positions transformed from purely factual power relations into a cosmos of acquired rights, and to know that [those rights] are thus sanctified."[12] The fact that human beings seem compelled to evaluate given political and economic arrangements in reference to sacred or cosmic standards suggests that religious and related beliefs play a special role in human experience and are more than simply the function of some prior material or external condition.

If religion and like beliefs were but the function of something else, it remains to be explained why conflicts over political legitimacy so readily and so recurringly get expressed in religious and similarly ultimate categories, and why those categories continue to have such wide and vital appeal. Why, exactly, does the struggle for dominance in so many places—in the Sudan, Sri Lanka, Tibet, Ukraine, Israel—have such a conspicuous and enduring religious dimension?

These considerations support the importance of attending explicitly to religious and similar beliefs in a study of intolerance while not losing sight of whatever conditioning circumstances are found to be relevant. This sort of orientation seems important in respect to understanding not just the sources of intolerance, but also the means for modifying or eliminating them.

One way of refining this kind of investigation is to develop a typology of possible relations between belief and intolerance that accommodates and helps to clarify the complexity of subject matter that has already been alluded to. The following is a preliminary attempt.

The general distinction between belief as a *target of* intolerance and belief as a *warrant for* intolerance is suggested by what have been called the twin principles of the UN Declaration against Intolerance: the principle of "the freedom to manifest religion or belief, stated in Article 1," and the principle of "the freedom from discrimination based on religion or belief, set forth in Article 2."[13]

The first principle is designed to protect people from becoming targets of intolerance—that is from being disadvantaged, confined, or injured for holding and expressing certain beliefs and for performing certain practices. While the way beliefs and practices are perceived varies according to circumstance, three general categories of belief as a target of intolerance may be enumerated: the unorthodox, the politicized, and the seditious.

The first category, *unorthodox belief,* refers to a religious or ideological belief perceived as intolerable from the point of view of the orthodox belief system. The second category, *politicized belief,* refers to a religious or ideological belief perceived as threatening the existing polity simply by virtue of recommending an alternative government structure or character. *Seditious belief,* finally, refers to a religious or ideological belief perceived as constituting incitement to active rebellion against an existing government.[14]

The second principle of the UN Declaration against Intolerance is designed to prevent people from using religion as a warrant for perpetrating acts of intolerance—that is, disadvantaging, confining, or injuring others in the name of a certain religion or belief. Belief as a warrant for intolerance refers to a belief held by a dominant group that is taken to entitle that group to act intolerantly toward others.

Primary Concerns of the Study

Sensitive to these categories and distinctions, this study has been conceived in light of three primary concerns:

1. To identify the character and degree of intolerance in each respective setting: Is belief the target of discrimination or persecution or both? What sort of belief is targeted (unorthodox, politicized, seditious)? What form does discrimination or persecution take? Is belief a warrant for discrimination or persecution?

2. To identify and analyze the justifications (religious or nonreligious) for intolerant treatment, as well as the responses of those subject to such treatment. (Here the various connections among belief and political legitimacy, ethnic identity, and national identity would be relevant.)

3. To determine the degree to which existing beliefs (and their justifications) may be treated more tolerantly if they are the target of intolerance and may become more tolerant or ''pluralistic'' if they are a warrant for intolerance.

Ukraine

Eastern Europe

From *Maps on File*. Copyright ©1987 by Martin Greenwald Associates. Reprinted with permission of Facts on File Inc., New York.

one

An Introduction to Ukraine

Ironically, the sudden and unexpected opportunities for religious liberty and pluralism created by glasnost have brought into the open long-repressed controversies that were produced or exacerbated by past policies. Those controversies now impede freedom of worship and the growth of mutual respect and peace among believers, as well as obstruct the achievement of a more just and peaceful political environment for Ukraine.[1] No matter how open the future may seem, it is hard to restructure history.

The new opportunities, the new thinking, *are* breathtaking. Mykola Panasovych Kolesnyk, chairman of the Council for Religious Affairs and the man with major governmental responsibility for religious life in Ukraine, leaves no doubt that Gorbachev's candid condemnation of standard Soviet policies concerning church life, and his departures from those policies, are now official.[2] There is, he says, no excusing the "multitude of follies" perpetrated against the Ukrainian people after the October Revolution and especially during the Stalin and Khruschev years. The closing of churches and monasteries, the widespread destruction of ecclesiastical buildings, the cruel suppression of religious exercise, and the "rude ideological attacks against religion" are all cause for shame.

Whatever the reasons propelling these policies, they amounted, on this account, to "an essential infringement of the freedom of conscience." Today, few defend the incompatibility of religion and communism. Rather, people would in general echo Gorbachev's sentiments about a "common history shared by atheists and believers alike," and "about the faithful being just Soviet people, workers, and patriots having every right to express their beliefs with dignity."

Official policy, as Kolesnyk describes it, is that these radically new attitudes toward religion lie "not only in accepting religious freedom, but also in affording practical support to such freedom." These changes have been particularly dramatic since June 1988, and the millennial celebration of the Christianization of the early eastern Slavic state Kievan Rus'. By now, three thousand religious communities, including Orthodox, Roman Catholics, numerous Protestant groups, Jews, Muslims, and a few others, have been legalized in Ukraine. Two thousand buildings formerly closed or put to secular purposes have been opened for religious use, and one thousand or so communities have been issued permits to build new houses of worship or to reconstruct old ones. Kolesnyk reports that, thanks to this new approach, there are in Ukraine some nine thousand active religious centers, including important historical cites and architectural masterpieces.

Experts generally agree, then, that religious believers in Ukraine, as throughout the Soviet Union, have benefited in varying degrees from glasnost and perestroika.[3] The new opportunities for freedom of exercise have been accompanied by the release of nearly all prisoners of conscience in 1986–88, by the removal or serious reduction of political and legal sanctions against religious expression, and by the relaxation of restrictions on the religious participation and education of children.[4] Nor is there extensive evidence of anti-Semitism in Ukraine these days.[5]

What is more, a new law on freedom of conscience in the Soviet Union has recently been adopted by the Soviet legislature, a law that ratifies the new policies toward religion being undertaken in the Soviet Union.[6] Even in its more liberal phase, Soviet religious policy had been applied by means of administrative decrees and regulations rather than by legislation. The thirty-one articles of the new law supersede long-standing Soviet policy and give juridical standing to registered religious bodies (article 13), together with the legal right to own property (article 18). They also permit the production and distribution of religious items and literature (articles 22 and 23), as well as the rights to maintain and use places of pilgrimage and to engage in charitable activities (article 24).[7]

The emphasis on the rights of religious freedom as sovereign guarantees conforms to Gorbachev's opinion, stated at the Nineteenth Party Conference in June 1988, that basic rights are not a gift from the state but are "an inalienable characteristic of socialism."[8]

At the same time, these very liberating developments have exposed deep-seated and long-suppressed antagonisms of a most profound and complicated sort among religious groups in Ukraine. As the state has relaxed its oppressive policies toward religion and permitted the legalization of hitherto suppressed churches, members of these churches suddenly find themselves required to confront old antagonisms.

The antagonisms have of late erupted into hostile acts among some of the groups, along with mutual accusations of discrimination and violence. These manifestations of intolerance certainly impede the process of creating a just and peaceful order within Ukraine. But, just as important, they frustrate the process of redefining in more equitable and agreeable terms Ukraine's relation to the other republics in the Soviet Union and primarily to the Russian Republic.

Ukraine is home to adherents of various religious denominations, not all of whom are involved in the conflict. There are numerous Protestant groups such as Baptists, Evangelicals, Pentecostalists, Seventh-Day Adventists, and Jehovah's Witnesses, along with Roman (Latin rite) Catholics, Jews, Muslims, and others. The present hostilities primarily involve three churches of the Eastern Byzantine tradition: the Ukrainian Catholic church (also called Greek Catholic or Uniate), the Ukrainian Autocephalous Orthodox church, and the Russian Orthodox church (the Ukrainian branch of which has recently been renamed Ukrainian Orthodox). Each claims descent from and continuity with the church of Kievan Rus', which was founded by means of a general baptism that took place in Kiev in the tenth century.

The issues that divide the churches stem both from theological and ecclesiological differences and from conflicting historical interpretations of national identity. Thus have religion and nationalism become inextricably intertwined in the current confrontation.

two

Religion and Nationalism
The Historical Setting

In 988, the grand prince of Kiev, Vladimir, proclaimed Christianity the official religion of his realm and had the inhabitants of Kiev baptized. The adopted form of Christianity was Byzantine, and the new church came under the authority of the patriarch of Constantinople, who was thereby entitled to appoint the metropolitans, or superior church leaders, of Kiev. With the division of Christendom in 1054 between the Catholic West and the Orthodox East, the Kievan church remained in the sphere of Byzantine Orthodoxy and in dependency on the patriarch of Constantinople.

During the twelfth and thirteenth centuries, the Kievan state (Rus') gradually disintegrated into a growing number of ever-smaller principalities, hastened by a series of Mongol invasions. As the result, the center of political gravity shifted away from Kiev. To the northeast, in the heartland of what was later to become Russia, the princes of Moscow (eventually called tsars) increased their power and extended their sovereignty. To the southwest, on the territory of Galicia in western Ukraine, another strong principality with a different political culture developed around the city of Halych, to be absorbed in the fourteenth century by Poland. Most of present-day Ukraine and all of Belorussia—together known as the Ruthenian Lands, from the Latin form of Rus'—fell under the rule of the Grand Duchy of Lithuania.

These political developments had important ecclesiastical repercussions. In 1299, the metropolitan of Kiev migrated northward and finally settled in Moscow. Maintaining the title "metropolitan of Kiev and all Rus'," he claimed jurisdiction over the Orthodox population of Lithuania. Lithuanian rulers, themselves Catholic and frequently in conflict with Moscow, disputed these claims. They at times convinced the patriarch of Constantinople to appoint a metropolitan different from the one residing in Moscow, although also with the title "metropolitan of Kiev." The deep jurisdictional conflict finally led to an ecclesiastical split after 1448. The church headed by the Moscow metropolitan declared its independence of the patriarch of Constantinople and laid the foundation for a separate Russian Orthodox church, which was made final in 1598 with the establishment of the patriarchate of Moscow. The Russian church continued to consider itself the rightful heir and representative of Kievan Christianity. In opposition, the metropolitans of the Grand Duchy of Lithuania maintained their loyalty to Constantinople, insisting that they were the legitimate descendants of Kiev.

It should be noted that during this period a partial, short-lived union of Western and Eastern churches was achieved at the Council of Florence in 1439. Even though it failed, it is important because it would serve as a prior historical warrant for the union that eventually did take place more than 150 years later between Rome and the Ruthenian (Ukrainian-Belorussian) Orthodox church. The Union of Florence, like subsequent similar efforts, was firmly rejected by the Moscow authorities, signaling a dispute and division in the church that would deepen further by the end of the sixteenth century.

In 1569, the Grand Duchy of Lithuania joined with Poland to form the Polish-Lithuanian Commonwealth. At the Council of Brest in 1596, the Ruthenian church, which was now located within the new commonwealth, officially united with the Roman church, thereby formalizing its separation from Russian Orthodoxy.

Under the terms of the Union of Brest, as it was called, the Ruthenian church accepted the primacy of the Roman pontiff as well as certain Catholic creedal and doctrinal formulations. Chief among these was the Catholic version of the Nicene Creed, according to which the Holy Spirit is said to proceed "from the Father and the Son" (filioque), rather than, as in the Orthodox version, from the Father alone. In turn, the Uniate or Eastern Rite Catholic church, as it became known, was permitted to retain its traditional administrative structure, its ancient Byzantine liturgy and rites, the use of Church Slavonic as the liturgical language, its discipline (including a married clergy), and equality with Roman Catholics in the Polish-Lithuanian Commonwealth.

The causes of the Union of Brest were numerous and complex and are still disputed. It is commonly agreed that the Orthodox church under Polish-Lithuanian rule was in a state of internal decay, afflicted by a number of abuses including simony, nepotism, and lax morality among the clergy. Bishops often were in conflict with the laity over the control of institutions. The Catholic church, by contrast, ascendant in the vigor of the Counter Reformation, launched an offensive with the support of Catholic rulers against which the Orthodox were poorly prepared to defend. Further, Jesuit schools attracted many Orthodox students, often leading to outright conversion. Accordingly, union with Rome held out a certain attraction, especially for the bishops and nobility, many of whom were Catholics already.

The Union of Brest was supported by a majority of bishops and some clergy, nobility, and burghers. It was vigorously opposed, however, by two bishops, much of the clergy, some nobility and burghers, and most of the peasants. And it was violently resisted by the Cossacks, who formed a society of free-lance warriors that emerged around this time in the area that is now south-central Ukraine. The Cossacks soon became zealous defenders of

Orthodoxy. Coercion, violence, and bloodshed, inflicted on all sides, escalated, and all attempts at healing the split and stopping the hostilities proved unsuccessful. The division was rendered permanent.

The struggle over the Union of Brest continued throughout the seventeenth century. Its abolition was one of the major demands of the great Cossack revolt against Poland in 1648. In 1654, the newly established Cossack state signed a treaty with Moscow that set the stage for the eventual domination of Ukraine by the Russian tsar and the extension of Orthodox influence in the region. In 1667, Ukraine was partitioned between Poland and Muscovy, and although the Union survived in the Polish or western section, it was abolished in the eastern part that was under Muscovite control.

Uniate territory was further restricted in the eighteenth century when Russia (as it was now known) advanced the cause of Orthodoxy by extending its sovereignty as a result of the partitions of Poland (1772–95). Eventually, the Uniate church survived only in the westernmost part of Ukraine, in Galicia and Transcarpathia, under Catholic Austrian rule. Nevertheless, by World War I, the Uniate church (now officically called Greek-Catholic) had become closely identified with the national identity of its Ukrainian adherents, a trend intensified in the interwar period when Galicia was ruled by Poland.

Although Orthodoxy was preserved in the part of Ukraine under Russian dominion, it gradually lost its national character. In 1686, the Ukrainian Orthodox church was transferred from the jurisdiction of the patriarch of Constantinople to the patriarchate of Moscow. By the beginning of the nineteenth century, the church hierarchy became totally Russian, at the direction of the patriarch of Moscow, and Ukrainian usages, traditions, and even architectural style were eliminated. Increasingly, the Russian Orthodox church was used by the tsarist regime as an instrument of denationalization of Ukrainians, whose very existence as a separate people was denied in the Russian Empire.

The Marxist-Leninist Background

Present religious strife in Ukraine is incomprehensible apart from Marxist-Leninist thought—as applied, it must be emphasized, in terms of Stalin's brand of Russian nationalism. Even though the influence of Marxism-Leninism is now sharply waning, if not disappearing altogether, it played a critical role in shaping the legacy of intolerance, the effects of which are still being felt.

According to conventional Marxism-Leninism, belief serves both as a warrant for and as a target of intolerance. The chief doctrines of Marxism-Leninism authorize the conviction that religious belief is the product of a perverse illusion, which, like any pathological idea, needs to be dispelled. To understand reality according to the tenets of dialectical materialism is to know that religion provides a bogus solution to a genuine problem. Human beings do suffer from the maldistribution of property and wealth and from the exploitation and victimization of the have nots by the haves. However, it is a grave mistake to seek otherworldly deliverance from abuses that have a decidedly this worldly cause. The beginning of wisdom is the exposure and elimination of such erroneous belief.[1]

Above all, religion must not be tolerated. It must be resisted by strenuous measures, because by concealing the real source of human suffering and thereby helping to preserve the position of the dominant classes, it is itself a means of exploitation and victimization.[2]

For this reason, both Marx and Lenin denounced as a bourgeois hoax the notion of freedom of conscience and, by implication, all the special moral and legal protections entailed in the notion. The thought of tolerating "all possible kinds of religious freedom of conscience" was for Marx obnoxious. The proper objective is "rather to liberate the conscience from the witchery of religion."[3] And for his part, Lenin belittled the suggestion that Communists might regard religion as a private matter, as a matter of individual conscience not to be interfered with even in the name of advancing their cause. Such a proposal lowers "the party of the revolutionary proletariat to the most vulgar 'free-thinking' philistine level...[by] renouncing all *party* struggle against the religious opium which stupefies the people" (emphasis added).[4]

Of special interest is Lenin's conviction that what he described as "refined" or "modernized" religion represented a greater threat to bolshevism than heavier-handed and more superstitious forms of religion. The former "substitute[s] more subtle and more advanced methods of stupefying the people"; it does "its work in a self-governing parish" and accordingly replaces "methods which are too crude, too antiquated, and too played-out to achieve their purpose.... The advocacy of one of the most vile things existing in the world—religion—and the attempts to replace the official priests by priests of moral conviction, represents the cultivation of the most subtle and, therefore, most loathsome kind of clericalism."[5]

Commitments to nationalism are also rejected by Marx and Lenin. In the words of the *Communist Manifesto*, "national differences and antagonisms between peoples are daily more and more vanishing" as the result of freedom of commerce and widespread participation in the world market. "The supremacy of the proletariat will cause them to vanish still faster.... In proportion as the antagonism between classes within the nation vanishes, the hostility of one nation to another will come to an end."[6] However useful loyalties to the modern nation-state may be in helping to develop human consciousness, such loyalties must ultimately be transcended by a universal awareness that is free of class and national limits. The entire thrust of Lenin's *State and Revolution* is the ultimate abolition of the modern nation-state, which, by generating an elaborate bureaucratic and military apparatus, has thereby increased "repressive measures against the proletariat, alike in the monarchical and the freest republican countries."[7] It follows, of course, that beliefs in the legitimacy of national identity, like religious beliefs, must be put aside.

In short, belief is here pitted against belief. Marxist-Leninists themselves believe that religious belief is harmfully mistaken and nationalistic belief ultimately regressive. As an expression and affirmation of the class antagonisms of material life, such beliefs may properly be targeted for active resistance. Accordingly, religious and nationalistic convictions are considered intolerable for being a noxious combination of unorthodox, politicized, and seditious beliefs:[8] they enslave the mind to superstition, they protect vested interests against political progress, and, "counterrevolutionary" in their nature, they represent a constant threat of violence against the Communist order.[9]

This theoretical opposition to religion and nationalism was reenforced, expanded, and in certain respects adjusted after the 1917 revolution by the Bolsheviks and subsequent Soviet governments.[10] From the beginning, religious believers were explicitly discriminated against: clerics lost their rights as citizens; they were denied state employment; their children were excluded from school beyond the elementary level and, in 1921, religious instruction of individuals younger than eighteen was declared illegal. Church property was nationalized and leased back to churches by the state under the most restrictive conditions. Beyond that, the state engaged in an active policy of religious persecution: "Between 1918 and 1920, at least twenty-eight bishops were murdered, thousands of clerics were killed or imprisoned, and an estimated 12,000 laypersons were put to death for religious activities. Thousands suffered arrest, trial, and deportation to labor camps or exile."[11]

As to his nationalities policy, Lenin pretended to favor Ukrainian independence, and in 1917 he officially recognized Ukraine as a sovereign state. At the same time, he undermined the independent government by helping to establish Communist control in 1920 under the guise of self-determination. In December 1922, after several years of armed conflict between Communist forces and Ukrainian separatists, Ukraine was compelled to join the other Soviet republics in creating a federal Soviet Union.

Stalin's Adjustments

The several objectives of Stalin's religious and nationalities policies during the twenties, thirties, and forties were not entirely consistent. There was a continuing campaign of religious suppression. In the 1920s and early 1930s, that campaign was aimed particularly at the Russian Orthodox church, which, by allying itself with the Whites during the revolution and by continuing to defy Soviet religious legislation, incurred Stalin's special wrath. Accordingly, Stalin intensified the campaign against Russian Orthodoxy in the 1930s by closing numerous churches, killing or confining thousands more clerics, and brutally suppressing religious activity.[12]

Prior to Stalin's rule, Lenin, despite his generally intolerant posture toward religion, was lenient with nationally identified religious movements. The objective was, no doubt, to undermine the hold of Russian Orthodoxy in places like Ukraine and to attract support in areas where bolshevism was still relatively weak.[13]

Reflecting that attitude, Soviet Ukrainian authorities gave some encouragement to the Ukrainian Autocephalous Orthodox church, which came into being in October 1921. The church expressly declared its independence from Russian Orthodoxy and what it regarded as the pattern of ''episcopal autocracy'' that worked to suppress legitimate Ukrainian interests and aspirations in favor of Russian domination. Most significant, the Autocephalous church repudiated the act in 1686 by which the Moscow patriarchate had assumed authority over the church centered in Kiev. Orthodoxy in Ukraine was now sharply divided along national lines. At the same time, the official attitude toward the Autocephalous church changed rather quickly. By 1923, indulgence had already begun to turn to hostility.

In 1929, Stalin abruptly launched a broad-scale attack on religion. He suppressed the Autocephalous church and liquidated its hierarchy and many of its clergy as counterrevolutionary and for espousing ''bourgeois nationalism.'' This maneuver was part of

Stalin's general effort to crush nationalist movements in the name of building a multinational Soviet state.[14] The enforced collectivization of Ukrainian farms in 1932–33, causing famine and the death of well over five million Ukrainians, and the campaign of terror that lasted until the end of the decade were aspects of the same general policy. In 1939, Stalin annexed western Ukraine and western Belorussia, making them part of the Soviet Union.

What was distinctive about Stalin and rather deviant from Marx and Lenin was his emphasis on amalgamating communism with Russian nationalism and undertaking to Russify the non-Russian republics such as Ukraine. This adaptation of Communist thinking was undoubtedly encouraged by World War II and the perceived need to mobilize a defense against Germany's threat to the Soviet homeland.

Ukraine was occupied by Nazi forces from 1941 to 1944. After they were driven out, a climate of relative relaxation temporarily prevailed in the region. But by March 1945, Stalin intensified his antireligious campaign, contending that during the war Ukrainians had not manifested sufficient loyalty to "the Soviet Fatherland." Particularly to blame were western Ukrainians, members of the Ukrainian Catholic church, who, it was alleged, engaged in treasonous collaboration with the German invaders in the interest of advancing Ukrainian independence. When Soviet troops took possession of Ukraine in 1944-45, there was no inclination to honor the spirit of Ukrainian nationalism. On the contrary, it was made clear that Soviet occupation was part of a strategy "to collect all Russian lands."

After the war, the Russification of Ukraine began in earnest. Russian was imposed as the language of instruction in the majority of institutions of higher education, and about half of the urban high schools were conducted in Russian. With respect to religious policy, Stalin began repressing the Ukrainian Catholic church. Then, collaborating with the Russian Orthodox hierarchy, he arranged the Synod of Lviv in 1946, which declared the "self-liquidation" of the Ukrainian Catholic church and its ''reunification'' with the Russian Orthodox church. There followed the arrest of the entire hierarchy, many clergy and faithful, and the transfer of some three thousand churches to the Russian Orthodox. All this was a direct outcome of Stalin's growing passion to remove any trace of commitment to Ukrainian independence.

It was Stalin's use of religion in his program of Russification that is particularly remarkable. His decision to reverse his earlier antipathy toward the Russian Orthodox church, to ''rehabilitate'' it, and to give it a constructive, if tightly restricted, role in fashioning a centralized Russian-Communist state marked a major adjustment in standard Marxist-Leninist thinking.

> Epitomizing its role of integrating above all the ''younger brothers''—Ukrainians and Belorussians—with the Russian ''backbone'' of the empire, the Orthodox Church is the only Union-wide multinational institution in the Soviet Union that has retained its pre-revolutionary name (''Russian'') as well as it ''monarchic'' (Patriarchal) centralized structure; . . . In its limited sphere, the Russian Orthodox Church symbolically represents what the Soviet leaders apparently conceive to be the essence of the ''new historical entity''—the ''Soviet people''—the ''merger'' of the Ukrainians and Belorussians with the Russians into a new ''Rus.'' On this kind of ''merger,'' there is, it seems, a fundamental agreement between the Patriarchate and the Kremlin and a broad consensus linking the regime and most Russians within and outside the USSR.[15]

three

Beliefs in Conflict

The acquiescence of the Russian Orthodox hierarchy to Stalin's policy of accommodation resulted from a variety of motives and considerations.[1] There was an elementary interest in the survival of the church, made understandable by the experience of severe persecution during the 1920s and 1930s[2] (not to mention the renewed antireligious campaign under Khrushchev in the early 1960s).[3] A strong measure of patriotic devotion to Russia, particularly during World War II, also helps to explain the willingness of the leadership to submit to Stalin's manipulation of the church for his own purposes.[4]

But, just as important, the Byzantine Christian tradition from which Russian Orthodoxy emerged laid the foundation for a cooperative or "symphonic" relation between church and state. The church typically provided legitimation for the emperor and for the integrity of the empire in exchange for civil protection of the church's monopoly over religious affairs. As one patriarch put it to the grand duke of Moscow in the late fourteenth century: "It is inconceivable for a Christian to have a church and not have a Tsar; for the state and the church are closely united and it would be impossible to separate them one from another."[5]

The Imperial Church: The Preferred Status of Russian Orthodoxy

The creation of a new and independent metropolitanate in Moscow in the mid-fifteenth century, which was elevated to a patriarchate in the late sixteenth century, gave to the interconnection of Orthodoxy and Russian nationalism a form fully in keeping with the tradition of the imperial church.

On this view, Russian identity is the natural and proper extension of the Kievan Rus' of the tenth century. Originally, the state called Rus' included East Slavic peoples now known as Ukrainians and Belorussians as well as the inhabitants of the territory to the northeast, the future heartland of the Russian state created by Moscow. The Ukrainians and Belorussians were believed to have been unnaturally severed from their Russian roots by Polish intervention. Moreover, just as these peoples all find their common ethnic identity in the Kievan Rus', so the Orthodox religion, introduced there in 988 and eventually centered in Moscow, is regarded as the authentic national religion of the region.

Stalin simply capitalized on this pattern of thinking in pursuing his own objectives. Subsequent Soviet policies, encouraging the pattern, have created in certain parts of the Soviet Union what has become ''to all intents and purposes. . .a state church.''

> It has very favorable coverage in sections of the Soviet press; it has hierarchs in the Soviet Parliament and several representatives in the Russian Parliament; its leaders were able to use their influence to effect the removal of Konstantin Kharchev from the post of chairman of the Council for Religious Affairs in June 1989; it is involved in a highly publicized way in social issues; priests are invited into the schools.[6]

Against this background, it was predictable that challenges to the authority of the Russian Orthodox hierarchy would be regarded, from the church's point of view, as properly subject to regulation and restraint by the civil authorities. Religious controversies and disputes were profoundly political matters and thus appropriately susceptible to political resolution.

It is this attitude that makes sense of the official Orthodox position concerning the dissolution of the national churches, such as the Ukrainian Catholics and the Ukrainian Autocephalous Orthodox. In both cases, the acts of dissolution were acts of state approved and embraced by the Russian Orthodox hierarchy.[7]

It is true that in January 1990 the Russian Orthodox church in the Ukraine was renamed the Ukrainian Orthodox church. This change involves the optional use of the Ukrainian language, a professed respect for indigenous cultural traditions, and provision for a local voice in the selection of Orthodox bishops.[8] On the other hand, the church is still juridically attached to the Moscow patriarchate, and for the present it seems impossible, to some observers at least, to regard the change as any more than superficial.[9] Whether there is potential for conflict between the Ukrainian and Russian Orthodox churches in response to ''the rising national sentiment in Ukraine'' remains to be seen.[10]

The Russian Orthodox Case against the Ukrainian Catholics

The Synod of Lviv of 1946, by which the Ukrainian Catholics were divested of all property and stripped of all rights to express and practice their religion, was, as mentioned, orchestrated by Stalin and his agents. The Orthodox hierarchy has generally celebrated the Synod as a ''joyful event [that] was possible only after the reunification of the Western Ukrainian population with the people of the Soviet Ukraine and the Soviet victory in the Great Patriotic War.''[11] In the words of Metropolitan Filaret, ''What triggered [the Synod]? Certainly not Stalin's repressions, which we all condemn, but the fact that the Uniate Church, which had set itself up artificially on captured territory in the Ukraine and Belorussia, had become outdated. Throughout its history believers saw this

unnatural union as a source of national, social and religious oppression."[12] As a scholar of the Russian Orthodox church succinctly
stated:

> Many [of the senior hierarchs of the Russian Orthodox church]
> are suspicious of the Catholic Church. They want to keep
> Orthodoxy as the pure, thousand-year-old source of spirituality
> and guardian of the Russian (and some surrounding) lands. To
> them, members of the Ukrainian Catholic Church are simply
> members of the Orthodox flock who fell into error and schism
> four centuries ago but, since 1946, have, happily, returned to the
> fold.[13]

The argument is that the Union of Brest of 1596, which produced
the Eastern Catholic church, was a thoroughly illegitimate or unnatural arrangement, one that was properly disowned and overturned by the Synod of Lviv.[14] It is claimed that the union with Rome
in the late sixteenth century was arbitrarily imposed on the faithful of Ukraine by the metropolitan of Kiev and a majority of Ukrainian bishops. They were, it is said, lured by material enticements
offered by Rome, as well as manipulated by the Polish king, who
was at the time in control of the territory.[15] Evidence of persecution
of the Orthodox by foreign Catholic rulers is often mentioned.

Above all, the Union of Brest represents for the Russian Orthodox a betrayal of the essentials of Orthodoxy. It maintains the outward form but not the spiritual substance of the tradition. Especially
is it indifferent to the history of outrages against Eastern Christianity
perpetrated by the pope and Western Christians. Beyond these
religious considerations, the alliance with Rome is also taken to be
a betrayal of a common ethnic tradition.

Accordingly, Metropolitan Filaret contrasts "the conditions of
political freedom and national unity" that existed after the Soviets
expelled the German forces in the 1940s with the "power of Rome"
and the Polish Jesuits by whose machinations the Union of Brest
had been "forced on our ancestors." And Patriarch Pimen declared
in 1986, "For forty years [since the beneficent achievements of the
Synod of Lviv], we have all been one common Orthodox family."

Other hierarchs echoed his belief that overturning the Union of Brest "put an end to enmity and hatred between brothers by blood."[16]

> Even now a certain number of people in [western Ukraine] stay under the Uniate influence, considering that the Union forcefully imposed on their ancestors, and not the Orthodoxy shared by our forefathers, is the true religion. . . . This causes us great sorrow. It is difficult to explain why certain priests and laity, . . .while keeping in mind the servility of the Uniate leadership toward the enemies of the Ukrainian people, are still unable to free themselves from the Uniate yoke. . . . Those believers. . .who are still in the Uniate captivity. . .should reunite with their Mother Orthodox Church. . . .[17]

The hierarchy have also alleged the "disloyalty" of Ukrainian Catholics in World War II by siding, it is asserted, "with the enemies of our Motherland." Metropolitan Filaret still speaks bitterly of those "who are believed to have given succor to the foe," particularly when he recalls the fate of his father, who was killed by the Germans during the war.[18] In 1945, the Orthodox position was represented by a leading Soviet anti-Catholic propagandist:

> Our Soviet state had inserted in its fundamental law the inviolable and unbreakable words about the freedom of conscience. It does not interfere with one's own religious conviction. But one cannot look on calmly, when the servants of the Uniate Church exploit this freedom of religion in order to engage in criminal activities against the Ukrainian people, in the interests of Fascist Germany in the past [and] today for the glory and benefits of the Anglo-Saxon imperialists. . . .[19]

Apart from the status of the Roman pontiff, the dispute between the Catholics and the Orthodox over whether or not to include the *filioque* phrase in reciting the Nicene Creed has been of historical importance. But however significant the dispute may have been in the past, there is considerable disagreement among contemporary observers over just how central this controversy, as well as other purely theological differences, is in the current conflict.[20]

Right up until December 1989, the Moscow patriarchate resolutely resisted the legalization of the Ukrainian Catholic church. Konstantin Kharchev, the former director of the Council for Religious Affairs, no doubt put it too strongly when he stated in July 1988 that the only obstacle to the official recognition of the Ukrainian Catholics was the "stern opposition of the Patriarchate."[21] In fact, the Soviet government itself was divided on the subject. Orthodox opposition was simply one cause among several for the government's reservations, reservations that were gradually overcome by Catholic pressure and by political developments in Ukraine.[22] Still, there was no mistaking official Orthodox antipathy to the Ukrainian Catholics.

In short, from the Russian Orthodox point of view, the Ukrainian Catholic church, for all the reasons cited, simply has no authority to exist. Given the preferred legal and political status Russian Orthodoxy takes to be its birthright, it had no difficulty approving an act of state in 1946 whereby a theological and historical judgment rejecting the validity of Ukrainian Catholicism is translated into a law that deprives Eastern Catholics of all civil rights. No spiritual legitimacy, no legal legitimacy.

The Russian Orthodox Case against the Autocephalous Church

During the recent millennial celebrations of the introduction of Christianity into Russia and neighboring areas (via Kiev), the late patriarch Pimen directed a message to the faithful outside the USSR, including those "who call themselves members of the Ukrainian Autocephalous church." He urged them to renounce separatism and join again with the mother church.[23] His call was rejected, but it set the tone for the celebrations, which were thoroughly Russo-centered. Almost no attention was given to the Ukrainian role in the spread of Christianity, nor to the significance of Ukrainian cultural and religious self-consciousness in the history of the area.[24]

Like the Ukrainian Catholic church, the Ukrainian Autocephalous church has been regarded as illegitimate by the Russian Orthodox. Indeed, because of controversies surrounding the consecration of Autocephalous bishops in 1921, it was so regarded by all forms of Orthodoxy. According to one Orthodox scholar, autocephalous priests abroad are not recognized by other Orthodox, nor is joint celebration of the liturgy allowed.[25] Moreover, like the Catholics, the Autocephalous are thought by the Russian Orthodox to have betrayed their religious and ethnic heritage as descendants of the Kievan Rus'.

Because Ukrainian Orthodox believers are considered by some to be schismatic, various acts of state that have on different occasions forcibly imposed the authority of the Moscow patriarchate have been embraced by the Russian Orthodox hierarchy. One such instance occurred after 1686, when the Russian tsar, having progressively annexed Ukraine to the Muscovite state, transferred church allegiance from Constantinople to Moscow, thereby incorporating the local Orthodox into the Russian church in the interest of "Pan-Russian unity."[26] Another was Stalin's suppression of the Autocephalous church in 1930 as part of his wider antinationalist campaign.

Accordingly, Russian Orthodoxy has itself become deeply involved in Ukraine, considering itself to be the authentic representative of Christianity there. Sixty percent of the Orthodox parishes registered in the Soviet Union are located in Ukraine.[27] The hierarchy is directly represented by means of the combined office of metropolitan of Kiev and exarch of Ukraine. The present incumbent, Metropolitan Filaret, is second in rank to the patriarch in Moscow and frequently represents the patriarchate abroad. The recent development of a Ukrainian branch of Russian Orthodoxy is but one more effort to secure the place of Orthodoxy in Ukraine.

This involvement is premised on a continuing claim to the exclusive authority of Russian Orthodoxy. There is no inclination to approve of the Ukrainian Autocephalous Orthodox church, nor to tolerate its legalization. The patriarchate has consistently "sought to put an end to the growing movement [of the Autocephalous church] in Ukraine and diaspora as a purely sectarian movement devoid of sacramental grace and canonical legitimacy."[28] In October 1989, after the Autocephalous church had declared its independence of Moscow earlier that year, a Russian Orthodox synod deposed and defrocked the first bishop of the new church, who had himself previously renounced his affiliation to the Russian church. It did the same in the case of a number of newly appointed Autocephalous priests.[29]

The Imperial Church and Civil Rights

According to one observer, the dispute between the Russian Orthodox and the Ukrainian Autocephalous Orthodox is "not...an issue of religious freedom or of human rights" in the civil-legal sense, but "an internal Orthodox matter," "a question of internal Orthodox canonicity."[30] The dispute concerns theological, historical, and ecclesiological matters of an in-house nature, matters that will have to be addressed and settled by the appropriate ecclesiastical authorities and jurisdictions. Certainly, it is possible to conceive of religious disagreements that do not affect civil liberties.

However, for the same reasons that the dispute with the Ukrainian Catholics involved more than questions of ecclesiastical significance, this dispute, too, touches on questions of civil legal and political importance—that is, broader questions of religious freedom and human rights. The reason is, at bottom, the imperial self-understanding of official Russian Orthodoxy.

The pervasive and deliberate interweaving of churchly and civil-political concerns inspired by Byzantine Christianity, nurtured by

Russian nationalism, and adapted by Stalinist imperialism disposed the Russian Orthodox hierarchy to welcome an arrangement in which ecclesiastical determinations directly entail civil-political consequences. Judgments internal to the church rejecting the "canonicity" of the Autocephalous movement and its claims to spiritual recognition and respect had a far-reaching effect, after the events of 1686 or 1930, on the movement's civil liberties. Thereafter, it was impossible for members of the Autocephalous movement to "have a religion or whatever belief" and "either individually or in community with others, and in public or private, to manifest [that] religion or belief in worship, observance, practice and teaching."[31] These effects occurred—in part, at least—because of basic and enduring convictions of the hierarchy. Just because of the set of official Russian Orthodox beliefs, the dispute over Autocephaly is at once an internal affair and an issue of religious freedom and human rights.

Accordingly, belief is once again pitted against belief. Now a set of theological and ecclesiological beliefs warrants, by implication, the legal suppression of unorthodox beliefs. The rejected beliefs targeted for suppression are seen, in addition, as likely to pose a political threat and even a potential threat of sedition.[32] However, in the case of Russian Orthodoxy, it appears that unorthodox belief is in itself extremely damaging and constitutes sufficient basis for "nullification" or "impairment" of the recognition, enjoyment or exercise of human rights and fundamental freedoms on an equal basis.[33]

The "Independent Thinkers"

The beliefs of the senior hierarchs in the Russian Orthodox church, while significant for being official, are not necessarily representative of the church as a whole. Many nonconformists, or dissidents, are sympathetic to the national church movements and welcome legalization, some of them going so far as to join those movements. "Despite the bishops' hostility, individual local Orthodox priests responded positively to Uniate appeals and participated in massive public religious services. Eventually, several of them either joined the Ukrainian Catholic Church or declared themselves adherents of the banned Ukrainian Autocephalous Church."[34] Others, while not quite so enthusiastic, are prepared to accept what they take to be inevitable. Still others are talking openly about the possibility of transferring membership to the Russian Orthodox church in exile, located in the United States.[35]

Many of these dissidents have rejected the official government and Orthodox account that challenges the legitimacy of the national churches. The claim, for example, that the Greek-Catholics voluntarily surrendered their distinctive identity at the Synod of Lviv in 1946 has never been accepted. Nor has the argument that the advocates of an independent form of Orthodoxy deserve persecution. Frequently, too, the dissidents have developed special respect and admiration for the members of the dispossessed religious groups who have persevered in their faith against severe odds.

Whatever their particular emphasis or angle of vision, independent thinkers "are referring more and more insistently to the inadequacies of the present leadership and calling for reform" (p.12). Such criticism appears to be creating resentment and a sense of intransigence on the part of the senior officials. The rapidity with which Patriarch Pimen was replaced after his death was initially seen as evidence of a renewed vitality among the hierarchs after a period of considerable inertia and lack of direction as the result of Pimen's bad health. But some are now interpreting this burst of activity as the bishops' attempt to protect their authority and initiative by controlling internal church politics, even at the local level, thereby giving less opportunity for the voice of the clergy and laity to be heard.

Moreover, there are reports of attempts by the hierarchy to curb activist, independent-minded priests, who are seizing new opportunities for educational and social work, participating in secular reform politics, and the like. There is some fear that by attracting attention and support, such priests might begin to undermine the authority of the existing officials (p. 12).

> I do think that [many of the dissidents and other groups who are criticizing or turning away from the Russian Orthodox hierarchy] are in search of freedom and greater democracy within the church. They are beginning to discover that changes can be made in political life, however slowly and painfully. Unpopular functionaries from a bygone era can be voted out of office, however much they try to stack the cards in their favor. Surely, people must now be asking why that cannot happen in the church? [p. 13].

The Defense of the Ukrainian Catholic Church

The Ukrainian Catholic pattern of belief relevant to questions of intolerance and discrimination is essentially reactive and dissentient. Ukrainian Catholics refuse to accept assertions of imperial authority by the Russian Orthodox church and the Soviet state and its predecessors. Traditionally unpersuaded by such claims, they see no reason why their long-standing loyalties to Rome and to an independent spiritual and ethnic identity and consciousness should not be respected and their desire to affirm and live by their convictions tolerated.

Ukrainian Catholics are less inclined to engage in disputation with the Russian Orthodox over the interpretation of their origins in 1596 at the Union of Brest than to affirm their right to interpret their origins as they see fit and to draw whatever lessons for belief and practice as seem to them compelling. They do not require universal acquiescence to their understanding and belief, simply the opportunity to follow that understanding and belief without civil interference or interference from other religious bodies.

There are important differences over historical understanding between Ukrainian Catholics and their opponents. However, a more immediate subject of dispute is the interpretation of the Synod of Lviv of 1946. Contemporary Ukrainian Catholics dissent sharply from the Russian Orthodox account. Far from being regarded as a ''joyful event,'' which made possible at long last the dissolution of the ''artificial'' and ''unnatural'' Uniate church and the consequent reunion of ''one common Orthodox family,'' the synod is regarded as thoroughly illegitimate and fraudulent. It was contrived by Stalin with the full complicity of the Russian Orthodox hierarchy for indefensible ecclesiastical and political objectives, and it resulted in the systematic nullification of the rights of conscience and free exercise for Ukrainian Catholics and in a policy of extreme persecution against them.

The following account of the synod constitutes the heart of the contemporary Ukrainian Catholic defense of itself and of its side of the present conflict.[36] The synod was arranged by the Moscow patriarchate with the approval of Stalin and other government officials to produce the illusion that the dissolution of the union with Rome and the ''return'' to the Russian church was ''voluntary'' and ''canonic.'' Because all Catholic bishops were in prison at the time, a sponsoring group for the ''Reunion'' was made up in May 1945 of intimidated Catholic clerics, who in February 1946 were subsequently received into the Orthodox church. From this group, two clerics were ordained without publicity as Orthodox bishops for Galicia, and they, masquerading as Catholics, convened and directed the synod. Thus, no authentic Catholic official was, in fact, a member of the sponsoring group.

> The ''Reunion'' [synod] which met in Lviv from March 8 to 10, 1946, bore all the marks of careful stage management. The date was selected to coincide with the 350th anniversary of the Union of Brest. There were no elections of delegates held in advance, nor were the agenda and rules of the [synod] previously published. Indeed, it appears from the proceedings of this gathering, that this very event was withheld from public knowledge until the [synod] had completed its task. Participation was on invitation of the ''Sponsoring Group,'' with the 216 clerical and 19 lay ''delegates'' lodged in selected hotels and transported in groups to and from the Sobor sessions. Besides the representatives of the Moscow

Patriarch, Soviet movie operators and press reporters were also on hand to record the proceedings in Lviv's St. George's Cathedral. If any of the participants still held any hopes for the Union, these were dispelled on the eve of the [synod] by the well-timed announcement by the Soviet [authorities] which doomed the imprisoned bishops of the Church. Conveniently dispensing with procedural niceties, the leaders of the "Sponsoring Group" appointed themselves as the presidium of the [synod] and announced its agenda. After several hours of speeches by the leaders of the "Group" and a "discussion". . .it was decided by an *open* vote to adopt the final decision on the future fate of the Church. The "Group" chairman. . .then presented the gathering with a draft resolution which was adopted without further discussion and by a unanimous show of hands. . . . [This document condemned the Union as something] "imposed upon our people in the sixteenth century by an aggressive Roman Catholic Poland as a bridge toward Polonization and Latinization. . . . [I]t would be unreasonable to support further Uniate tendencies and it would be an unforgivable sin to continue the hatred and fratricidal war within our people, of which the Union was the cause in history and must always remain so. . . ."

The expected outcome of the Lviv [synod] was followed by the equally predictable action of the Soviet authorities, which in effect gave the decisions of the [synod] the force of law in the entire Soviet territory. . . . After February, 1949, . . .the tried methods of "persuasion" were applied against the Greek Catholic "recalcitrants"—"conditioning" by the N.K.G.B. and mass arrests and deportations of those who failed to submit. . .their "declarations of conversion."

Throughout the Soviet Union, the priests of the "prohibited Church" who were still active were now rounded up and charged with "illegal" performance of sacerdotal functions, while all remaining Uniate monasteries were closed and converted to secular uses [and all other church property expropriated]. Whatever remained of the Greek Catholic Church in the USSR could henceforth subsist only in the "catacombs," or in the minds and consciences of the priests and believers camouflaged as converts to Orthodoxy.[37]

One other point of strong dissent concerns the interpretation of alleged Catholic cooperation with the Nazis during World War II. Although there is no doubt that Catholics played an important role in the massive nationalistic movement that emerged in 1941 with the retreat of the Bolsheviks before the invading German armies, there was little affection for the Nazis, particularly after they revealed their plans for Ukraine. Far from uniform collaboration, the record reveals a substantial degree of resistance, including the efforts of Metropolitan Sheptyts'kyi and others to save Jewish children.[38] Indeed, the Church's efforts to protect Jews were, it is said, as courageous as those of any church in Nazi-occupied Europe. Most important of all, after the German occupation had ended, it was standard Soviet practice to threaten all Catholic clergy with the charge of collaboration unless they would convert to Russian Orthodoxy.

Contrary to expectations, the Ukrainian Catholic church succeeded in maintaining itself surreptitiously against a campaign of suppression and persecution. Despite some defections to Orthodoxy, the clergy and laity endured because, in the eyes of many western Ukrainians, the Orthodox were "unable to shed an aura of illegitimacy both as a 'Muscovite' and a Soviet-imposed church."[39]

Basically, Ukrainian Catholics believe they are entitled to three things, as stated by Metropolitan Volodymyr Sterniuk, archbishop of Lviv, on March 17, 1990: (1) full recognition of the Ukrainian Catholic church as an independent juridical body, (2) return of all properties confiscated from the church, and (3) a formal declaration of the 1946 "pseudo-synod of Lviv" as "uncanonical."[40] The third demand underscores the centrality of the Synod of Lviv and the absolute need, from the Catholic point of view, to repudiate its spiritual authority. The first and second demands, if satisfied, would begin to rectify the civil effects of the synod by observing the institutional independence of the church and by providing restitution of expropriated property. They imply the state's direct accountability for the discrimination and persecution to which the church believes it was subjected.

> I think that there is an important role for the Soviet state, and in particular for the government of the Ukrainian SSR, to clearly declare the historical injustice [of the suppression of the Ukrainian Catholic Church and of the Autocephalous Church]—to declare that these acts, because they were illegal, because they violate Soviet and international norms, they are declared null and void, and the government has to accept responsibility to recognize the church that they have banned. . . [and grant restitution for historical injustice].[41]

The Ukrainian Catholic hierarchy has said that once the second condition has been met—the due return, by the state, of all confiscated property—then case-by-case negotiation may begin so as to make some allowance for the interests of the Russian Orthodox church. But such consideration would not, strictly speaking, be a matter of justice (because church properties were unjustly transferred to the Russian church in the first place). Rather, it would be a matter of equity or charitable concern on the part of the Catholics. Strictly speaking, the Russian Orthodox church has no basis for a claim of right, but only for an appeal, a plea, to the goodwill of the Ukrainian Catholics.

The Defense of the Ukrainian Autocephalous Orthodox Church

In support of its declaration of national independence from Russian Orthodoxy in October 1921, the Ukrainian Autocephalous church invoked the traditional ideals of conciliarism as its authority. These ideals began to take shape in the twelfth century within Western Christianity as part of a movement against papal absolutism.

Conciliarism emphasized the priority of constitutional and representative government within both church and state, the division of spiritual and temporal powers, and the sovereignty of ''the

people" in ecclesiastical and civil government. The authority of the
people refers not only to popular sovereignty but also to the idea
of defining ecclesiastical and civil jurisdiction in reference to the
territorial and cultural boundaries of a given people or nation. It
is from this second implication that the notion of nationalism in
regard to the organization of church and state takes on importance.

The Ukrainian Autocephalous share the belief with the Russian
Orthodox that because Christianity came to Kievan Rus' from
Byzantium under the authority of the patriarch of Constantinople
it was therefore Orthodox. They reject, however, the Russian interpretation of the ethnic character and identity of the original community. On that question they essentially agree with the Ukrainian
Catholics.

In that spirit, the synod that gathered at the Cathedral of St.
Sophia in Kiev in October 1921 agreed that the Ukrainian Orthodox were fully authorized to declare the national independence of
their church on the basis of a constitution that "shall henceforth
be popular and conciliar."[42] The synod understood the church to
have had an ancient and continuous existence, lacking only its own
hierarchy. Accordingly, it in effect "create[d] its own episcopacy"[43]
by invoking the "Alexandrine" privilege, whereby bishops might
be consecrated by the grace of the Church represented by its
assembled clergy and laity.[44] The organization would no longer be
arranged on a rigid hierarchical model, but composed of a "loose
hierarchy of lay-dominated, self-governing church councils (rady),"
in which all offices, including the bishops, would be elective.
Perhaps most significant of all, the synod repudiated the annexa-
tion in 1686 of the church centered in Kiev by the Moscow Patriarchate as "immoral," "anti-canonical," and an act of violence.
Without question, this declaration represents a radical break with
"the canonical status quo" (p. 321).

Four of the five principles that summarize fundamental
Autocephalous beliefs constitute a direct rejection of the imperial

image of church-state relations represented by the symphonic arrangement between Russian Orthodoxy and the Soviet state.[45]

First, the separation of church and state emphasizes "Christian freedom" and the independence of religious expression and exercise from civil interference.

> The church should be strictly apolitical. The church's efforts to obtain support and protection from the state, the resulting transformation of the church into a handmaiden of the state, a willing submission of the church to the exploitation by the state as a political factor, as well as hostile activities of the church against the state— [all these] are contrary to the nature of the church... [unless God's will contradicts the will of the state, in which case] we shall courageously carry out the will of God.[46]

Second, the principle of autocephaly, or "the ecclesiastical equivalent of the ideal of national independence from Russia,"[47] is obviously of central importance. After the Soviets crushed the short-lived Ukrainian State (1917–21), the church assumed an important role in the Ukrainian national movement. "The Autocephalists firmly believed that subordination to the Russian church was not compatible anymore with the state of national consciousness in the Ukraine and represented a major obstacle to the still unfinished task of nation-building and that autocephaly was a prerequisite for realizing such other goals of the movement as the Ukrainization and democratization of the church in the republic."[48]

Third, the principle of Ukrainization is based on the idea that valid religious experience requires expression in the culture and language of the faithful. There was an explicit effort to de-Russify church rites, traditions, religious art, and music as well as language. Folk music and art were now to be used in the liturgy, together with historic Ukrainian religious customs and traditions. Participation by "the people" in all aspects of worship, as of administration, was encouraged. "The once-ridiculed 'market language' of the common people, viewed as 'uncultured' and 'unfit' for sacral purposes, was. . .given a new sense of dignity and respect. According to the contemporaries, among the Ukrainian peasantry it was indeed the Ukrainian-language church services with their revived native rites and chants that offered the strongest attraction to the new church."[49]

Fourth, the principle of conciliar self-government was claimed to arise from the egalitarian, participatory practices of the primitive Christian communities. Only as the church amassed wealth, power, and privilege was it attracted to monocratic and clerically dominated patterns of organization. Russian Orthodoxy, accommodated as it was to the Soviet state, "ceased to be apostolic and became an imperial [church]."[50]

Despite the effects of persecution after 1930, remnants of the original Autocephalous church continued to exist in a clandestine way until 1942. Thereafter, the church reconstituted itself. While retaining its emphasis on independent national identity, it turned away from its conciliar and democratic image and adopted an episcopal system along conventional Orthodox lines. The cause of the Autocephalous church was kept alive by means of attacks on the Russian Orthodox hierarchy by underground newspapers such as the *Ukrainian Herald*. For example, in spring 1974, the *Herald* objected strenuously to external religious domination:

> And maybe the Exarch will tell us what he did with Father Sava of St Volodymyr's Cathedral in Kiev, after he began delivering his sermons in Ukrainian? Maybe he can also tell us why in 1972 only four students from the Lviv region were accepted into the Odessa Theological Seminary? Why an atmosphere of [Russian] chauvinism pervades the seminary? Why services in the churches of Ukraine are conducted in Russian, with the exception of the western regions, and even there not in all areas?. . . Why is there no religious literature published in the Ukrainian language? No, the Exarch will not answer these questions. We will do this for him. It is because there is no official Ukrainian Church in Ukraine. Moscow usurped the Ukrainian Orthodox Autocephalous Church in eastern Ukraine in the thirties and the Greek-Catholic Church in western Ukraine in the forties. Moscow's Orthodox Church is

an instrument of russification. Key administrative positions in the Church are held by obedient lackeys who care only about their earthly comforts and who receive a dole from the satanical regime for their black hypocritical deeds.[51]

It ought to be pointed out that although the name is the same, the Ukrainian Autocephalous Orthodox church that was reactivated in 1989 is very different from the church of 1921. The contemporary church has not adopted the reforms and the outlook characteristic of the Autocephalous movement in the 1920s, specifically the conciliar-democratic and lay-oriented form of church government. Rather, it follows the traditional Orthodox practice that, while still nationally independent, is strongly based on hierarchical and clerical structures.

On June 5–6, 1990, a synod of the Ukrainian Autocephalous Orthodox church, held in Kiev, established its own patriarchate. It elected Mstyslav Skrypnyk, metropolitan of the Ukrainian Orthodox church in exile in the United States, as the new patriarch with the title metropolitan of Kiev and all Ukraine.

In addition, the synod called for the return of church buildings, monasteries, and other assets that had belonged to the church before it was liquidated in 1930.[52] A special telegram was sent to the Russian Orthodox church reasserting that the Kievan metropolitanate had been ''forcibly'' and ''illegitimately'' annexed to Moscow in 1686, protesting the Russification of Orthodoxy in Ukraine by the Russian church, and demanding that the status of the Autocephalous church, as an independent Ukrainian Orthodox body, be fully recognized (p. 11).

Patriarch Mstyslav himself has underscored these concerns: ''Church history and secular history, in the case of Ukraine and probably other nations, are two things that cannot. . . be separated. It is only when one looks as these two together that one will come to a complete and full understanding of the intricacies of the national history. . . . During the tsarist regime, the Russian Orthodox church was an instrument of colonization.''[53]

Differences between the Ukrainian Catholic and the Autocephalous Orthodox Churches

The contemporary religious conflicts in Ukraine are not restricted to the age-old antipathy between the two national churches and the Russian Orthodox church. The Ukrainian Catholics and the Ukrainian Autocephalous are also at odds. Although they share a common interpretation of Ukrainian ethnic origins that sets them against the traditional Russian account, they divide, at bottom, over how their respective religions fit in with the Ukrainian heritage.

The lines are clearly drawn in an interview recently conducted with a leading prelate of the Ukrainian Autocephalous Orthodox church: Ioann, metropolitan of Lviv and Halych and locum tenens for Patriarch Mstyslav in his absence.[54] Metropolitan Ioann explains why clergy and laity are currently joining the Autocephalous church not only from the Russian Orthodox, as they are doing in large numbers, but also from the Ukrainian Catholic church, as, for example, in the Ivano-Frankivsk district "where six, seven parishes went over to the UAOC." He goes on to make some highly provocative and controversial remarks about the Ukrainian Catholics, remarks that illustrate well the inflammatory character of some parts of the dispute currently taking place between the two national churches.

> There never was a Greek Catholic Church traditionally. It was forcibly established. Until 1596 only the Orthodox Church was found there, and then under Poland's occupation the Ukrainian Greek Catholic Church was coercively formed on those lands. This church was not provided by the Ukrainian people, but it was an acquisition of Poland and Rome. And this is what the Ukrainian people are now beginning to realize.

> History is history; history cannot be changed, rewritten, or told in any other manner. Ukrainianism was preserved better in Orthodoxy; in Ukrainian Orthodoxy, not Moscow Orthodoxy. Moscow's Orthodoxy destroyed our traditions. Within the UAOC, our ancestral traditions that have their beginnings from the days of Volodymyr the Great, and not from Moscow, which enslaved our Church in 1687.

[It was] the Ukrainian Autocephalous Orthodox Church [that was able] to revitalize those good Orthodox traditions which were prevalent in the Cossack glory days, when our great hetmans fought for the Ukrainian Orthodox faith, for Ukraine.

Often the words of the Ukrainian national anthem come to mind: "The soul, the body, we will lay down [in battle] for our freedom and we will show that we are of Cossack stock." But how can we claim to be of Cossack stock when we do not carry their faith, the faith of the Cossacks, which they so staunchly defended [pp. 3, 14].

The tendency to bring Ukrainian Orthodoxy into close association with authentic national identity also appears in the words of Metropolitan Mstyslav: "We are the independent Church of the independent nation";[55] but it should be emphasized that both Metropolitan Mstyslav and Ioann defend the right of all to express and practice their beliefs freely and without discrimination.[56]

According to recent reports, Ukrainian Catholics perceive that their national loyalty is frequently challenged by some leaders and lay members of the Autocephalous church. They find themselves being described as "Polish agents" bent on reestablishing Polish and papal suzerainty over western Ukraine. Catholics reject such a characterization and reaffirm their devotion both to (Eastern) Catholicism and to Ukraine.[57]

As in their response to Russian Orthodox accusations of the "illegitimacy" of the Union of Brest, Ukrainian Catholics insist on the right to define their own origins and religious identity. They point out that the historical fears of supporters of Ukrainian Orthodoxy that union with Rome would lead to Latinization and Polonization proved unfounded. The Ukrainian Catholic Church over the centuries became closely identified with the national consciousness and aspirations of the Ukrainian nation and was a staunch defender of its national rights. Indeed, they emphasize that the Soviet regime and the Russian Orthodox Church routinely denounced the Ukrainian Catholic Church precisely for its connection with Ukrainian nationalism. They find ironic, and indignantly reject, therefore, imputations that the Ukrainian Catholic Church is paving the way for the return of Polish rule

and the Polonization of Ukrainians. In their turn, some Ukrainian
Catholics have branded the Autocephalous Orthodox as tools of
the KGB which hopes to weaken the Catholic Church and the
Ukrainian national movement. Here they point out that while the
Catholic bishops and clergy suffered an underground existence
and severe repression, many of the current leaders of the Autocephalous Church served loyally in the ranks of the Russian
Orthodox hierarchy and clergy until their recent espousal of
Autocephaly—which was made possible only by the weakening of
the Russian Orthodox position by the Catholics! They also view
with suspicion the fact the Autocephalous Church is directing its
energies not at the traditionally Orthodox areas of Eastern Ukraine,
where the Orthodox churches overwhelmingly maintain ties with
the Moscow Patriarchate, but at the traditionally Catholic areas of
Western Ukraine. These sharp polemics over religious and historical issues are further exacerbated by struggles over church properties much like those described above between the Ukrainian
Catholics and Russian Orthodox.[58]

four

The Strife of the Churches

The recent relaxation of government restraints on the exercise of religion has not only allowed the open discussion of issues and tensions long suppressed. It has also created a situation in which direct confrontation, sometimes breaking out in open hostility and intolerance, has occurred principally among adherents of the three churches whose beliefs we have just outlined.

The Russian Orthodox versus the Ukrainian Catholics

One locus of serious difficulty exists in the four southwestern *oblasti* or subdivisions of Ukraine (Transcarpathia and three other districts—Lviv, Ivano-Frankivsk, and Ternopil) that make up Galicia.

In December 1989, the government permitted the parishes of the Ukrainian Catholic church to register and to begin practicing their faith after having been forbidden to do so for forty-three years. After having lost some three thousand churches to the Russian Orthodox as the result of the Synod of Lviv in 1946, Ukrainian Catholics, legitimate once again, wanted back what they regard as their churches. Toward that end, they have begun to take things into their own hands in some places.

For their part, the Orthodox, after nearly a half century of administering the churches, are just as adamantly opposed to losing parishes they believe to be properly theirs. On occasion, they have employed irregular countermeasures to protect their interests. In general, the situation is as follows:

> The immediate response of Ukrainian Catholic believers to the belated, limited promise of legalization was the takeover of their former churches from the Russian Orthodox church. By early January 1990, 120 churches were seized in Galicia, and by the end of the month the number increased to 230 churches in the Lviv and Ternopil diocese, and 140 in the Ivano-Frankivsk diocese. By late spring, according to Ukrainian Catholic sources, approximately 400 churches were taken over by the newly formed, though still mostly unregistered Uniate parishes in the Lviv diocese, some 500 in the Ivano-Frankivsk eparchy, and 11 in Transcarpathia. Almost 400 priests followed their parishioners and joined the Ukrainian Catholic Church. This increased the strength of the Uniate clergy to nearly 800,[1] including 186 monastic priests and brothers.

> The mass takeover by the Ukrainian Catholics of their former churches evoked a flurry of protests from the Moscow Patriarchate, Exarch Filaret of Kiev, and the Orthodox bishops from Western Ukraine. They involved charges of the Uniate use of "violence" in the "illegal seizure of churches," "intimidation" of Orthodox believers, and "persecution of Orthodox clergy"—charges that were instantly publicized by some Soviet media. Spokesmen for the Russian Orthodox Church appealed to Gorbachev and law and order agencies for protection and help against the so-called "nationalist," "separatist extremists" in Galicia, who allegedly have masterminded and exploited for their political ends the Uniate resurgence which, the Patriarchate worried, is developing into a religious "civil war."[2]

Although there is some diversity of opinion within the church, a number of Russian Orthodox hierarchs have recently issued strong denunciations of what they take to be violent acts on the part of the Ukrainian Catholics. Early this year, the Bishops' Council sent a telegram to President Gorbachev urging his help in resisting "the acts of violence and lawlessness by Uniate extremists." Archbishop Kirill of Smolensk stated:

> What is happening in Western Ukraine is not a confrontation between Orthodox and Catholics, but more accurately a confrontation with an underlying nationalist cause, in which confessional ideas and religious ideas are being used to inflame the struggle. There is only one way out: to stop the violence. Violence cannot be the means of solving a problem, it will only throw everything into chaos. Violence is dangerous, because it always engenders violence in return. . . .[3]

Metropolitan Alexi of Leningrad, newly elected patriarch, spoke to the Congress of Peoples' Deputies on June 7, 1990, in no uncertain terms.

> Many deputies present here already know of the tragic events taking place in some regions of Western Ukraine. It is a matter of outrageous acts of lawlessness performed by people who call themselves adherents of the Ukrainian Catholic Church against Soviet citizens, Orthodox believers. . . . [D]ozens of Orthodox churches are being seized by force. Orthodox priests are being driven from their places of work, and ordinary believers, under threat of violence, are converting to the Uniate. . . . Arbitrary acts are being organized and carried out by people who can only very doubtfully be called believers. . . . The impression is being created that someone very much wants to make use of a difficult political situation to kindle tension in national relations in order to realize their own political ambitions.[4]

As reported in the Ukrainian press, Bishop Ionafan, secretary of the Synod of the Ukrainian Orthodox church and assistant to Metropolitan Filaret, said that tensions between the Russian Orthodox and the Catholics could result in a "spiritual Chernobyl" or a "Ukrainian Northern Ireland."

> During an April 11 [1990] meeting in Kiev with journalists, Bishop Ionafan read a synod declaration protesting the April 6 decision of the Lviv City Council to return St. George Cathedral to

Ukrainian Catholics. Catholics built the cathedral in the 1700s and worshipped there until their Church was outlawed by the regime of Josef Stalin. The declaration, which called the Lviv decision "a gross violation of the rights of Orthodox believers," was signed by all the bishops in the newly formed Ukrainian Orthodox synod, which is part of the Russian Orthodox Church. . . . All day long every day in Lviv, Orthodox believers gather in the cathedral courtyard for liturgy and prayers, while Ukrainian Catholics stand on the church steps with a crucifix propped against the doors to celebrate their services. The two groups pray simultaneously, drowning out each others' voices. A Ukrainian man with a black and blue bump on his forehead claimed to have been hit with a cane by an Orthodox woman. . . . Bishop Ionafan said the cathedral was closed because "there has been a blockade of warriors of the (Ukrainian) Catholic Church."[5]

Another report also describes the tensions generated over the transfer of St. George's Cathedral in terms of a "religious war."[6]

The scene in front of St. George's Cathedral in Lviv couldn't have been more poignant: two clutches of elderly women, screaming at each other in full voice, arguing over whether the cathedral belongs to the Russian Orthodox or the Ukrainian Catholics. . . . "I don't know why they're even bothering," said a young woman, herself entering the fray with occasional comment. "No one's going to convince anybody their side is right." The high-pitched debate, it turns out, was only a taste of things to come. . . . Within a matter of days, the cathedral grounds became the setting for the latest episode of Ukrainian religious conflict [p. 12].

Metropolitan Filaret of Kiev has had perhaps the strongest things to say.

A handful of people from a church they themselves closed have been trying to use the democratization processes underway in our country and religious liberty to revitalize the Uniate Church. Their main objective is to set up a "national church" in contrast to the Orthodox one. Nationalistic elements have been trying to use the Uniate Church to estrange Ukrainians from Russians, their half-brothers. . . . [G]atherings were held to propagandize the ideas of nationalism and cultivate hostility and hatred for the believers of other creeds, which is against the Constitution of the Ukrainian SSR. . . ?

Exhibiting the opposite point of view, one recent report describes widespread grass-roots resistance among Ukrainian Catholics to any resolution of the conflict until "the Orthodox leadership first turn over Ukrainian Church buildings and other property seized years ago by the state."[8] And a Ukrainian Catholic priest defends widespread agitation in favor of recovering church property as readily understandable, as "simply natural" and not the result of outside incitement. "The time has come; the time of restructuring has come, . . . and the people who were in agony up to now, feeling themselves to be [Catholics], and who have started work to revive the church, in no way. . . require any kind of [external encouragment]."[9]

The tone of the conflict is aptly captured by the following account.

> "During the night of 30–31 January of this year in the city of Sambor under threats from the Uniates, the authorities turned the Orthodox temple over to them. On 31 January at about 1900, the temple was surrounded by about 2,000 Orthodox believers and an ultimatum was given: If the Uniates do not release our temple the Orthodox will take it by force." On 1 February at 1300, another report was received from Sambor to the effect that the Orthodox had forced the Uniates out of the temple.[10]

Observers differ as to whether violence has actually been employed in the attempt to occupy church buildings. According to Jane Ellis, no detailed documentation of the allegations of violence exists, but it surely would have, "had specific incidents been reported. . . . Confrontations have certainly taken place, involving in some cases the threat of force or the use of force—but no specific case of actual violence has emerged."[11] To gain control of a church by threatening but not using metal objects, as has happened, is an example of the use of force. What have not been verified are acts of violence, in which people are actually beaten with those objects.[12] Father Alexander Webster does not find the distinction entirely convincing. "In any event, the blanket statement that there is not evidence for the claims of the Russian hierarchy is just too confident," and "tilts" too uncritically toward the Ukrainian Catholic position.[13]

At present, the law, according to Soviet authorities, favors the Orthodox because, as a result of the Synod of Lviv, Ukrainian Catholic churches and other properties were leased to the Orthodox, giving them exclusive title. The government believes it may break the leases and redistribute the churches now held by the Orthodox only under specified conditions: illegal use of the property by the occupants; willingness by the leaseholders to return their church to the state, to share it with others, or to relinquish it and build another; or willingness to submit the question to a local vote.[14]

In some instances, local votes have been tried and peaceful transfers have taken place. However, that procedure works only where there is unanimous support for one side or the other. In those cases—particularly in the cities, where both communions are represented and compete with each other for occupancy—"there is no resolution, and there is a lot of tension" (p. 5). One example is the decision of the Lviv city council to transfer the Cathedral of St. George to the Ukrainian Catholics in August 1990, a decision that continues to cause resentment among the Russian Orthodox hierarchy.

Nor is there much readiness on the part of Orthodox parishes, even those with a minority of worshippers, to relinquish a church to the Catholics and then construct a new building. "We are the ones with the lease, and we're not about to give up our cathedral we legally [hold] under Soviet law; it's ours, and even though there's a majority of Catholics, why should we go build, why should we spend our money?. . ." (p. 5).

In any case, whatever pragmatic arrangement is worked out from place to place, the law and central government policy, as they stand, staunchly favor the Russian Orthodox. Not only are the Orthodox given first option on the property; any occupancy achieved by the

Ukrainian Catholics remains unofficial. The government refuses to register any church as Ukrainian Catholic, for it has not yet recognized the Ukrainian Catholic hierarchy as legitimate.[15] It holds that given groups who happen, by one means or another, to gain control of a church may worship and organize the parish as they see fit. But from a legal point of view, the church is still officially Orthodox.

Catholics perceive this situation as grossly discriminatory. The fact that the law as it stands recognizes the right of the Orthodox as leaseholders to occupy church property[16] only proves, from a Catholic perspective, how unfair the law is. Catholics built these churches in the first place and then lost them by an arbitrary act of expropriation in 1946. Any law that ignores these facts is illegitimate. Catholic resentment would only intensify were there no promise of relief regarding the leasing policy.[17]

For their part, the Orthodox contend that they have faithfully tended the parishes for nearly fifty years and have thereby earned the right to continue. Moreover, they claim, there are now more Orthodox members than Catholics and they, therefore, should be given preference. This point, of course, is subject to considerable dispute.[18]

The Russian Orthodox versus the Ukrainian Autocephalous Orthodox

But if the conflicts between the Orthodox and the Catholics are an important part of the religious crisis in Ukraine, they involve more parties than simply these two. There is, in addition, the newly restored Ukrainian Autocephalous Orthodox church, which stands in strong tension with the Russian Orthodox church (and its Ukrainian branch) and may also represent something of a threat to the Ukrainian Catholics.

The legalization of the Autocephalous church has been met with strong resistance by the Moscow patriarchate,[19] no doubt partly

because of its potential for growth in areas of the Ukraine traditionally dominated by Russian Orthodoxy.[20] Strong objection has
been registered to the transfer of churches from the Russian Orthodox to the Ukrainian Autocephalous Orthodox. A recent press
report describes the revulsion of a Russian Orthodox priest in Lviv
concerning a proposal by city authorities to transfer the Church of
the Transfiguration to the Autocephalous. Calling the
Autocephalous church "satanical," he foresees a bloody conflict between members of the competing churches should the authorities
proceed with their plan.[21]

In a large number of parishes, priests have defected from Russian
Orthodoxy and joined the Autocephalous church, taking their
parishes with them.[22]

> At present [the Ukrainian Autocephalous Orthodox church] has
> parishes in all of the eastern Ukrainian oblasts. We hear news of
> six, seven, eight parishes daily in eastern Ukraine joining the
> ranks of the UAOC. Currently, I am informed we have over 1,000
> priests and over 2,000 church-parishes. . . . These priests come
> from the ranks of the Russian Orthodox Church; at present they
> are joining our Church in masses. I also have news that many of
> the bishops of the Russian Orthodox Church who hold eparchal
> posts in Ukraine, want to join the ranks of the UAOC.[23]

On October 28, 1990, the following event occurred in Kiev.

> Solemn divine service was conducted today in St. Sophia's
> Cathedral in Kiev. It was devoted to the announcement of self-rule
> and independence of the Ukrainian Orthodox Church. On this
> occasion Aleksiy II, patriarch of Moscow and all Russia, presented
> the blessed diploma to Metropolitan Filaret of Kiev and of all Ukraine.

> The Ukrainian Autocephalous Orthodox Church resolutely protested
> this action, seeing in it an encroachment on the national sovereignty
> of Ukraine. On its way to the cathedral, the patriarch's limousine
> was stopped by a group of believers of the [UAOC]. To demon-
> strate their protest, Ukrainian people's deputies Mykhaylo Horyn
> and Oles Shevchenko prostrated themselves on the asphalt in
> front of the cavalcade. However, personnel of the law and order
> agencies picked them up and pushed them into the crowd.

Clashes occurred in the square between participants in the demonstration and militiamen. The confrontation between believers of these two churches outside St. Sophia's Cathedral lasted throughout the day. A group of Ukrainian people's deputies and delegates of the all-Ukrainian Assembly of Rukh appeared live on Ukrainian television with their evaluations of events outside the Cathedral.[24]

The statement by the members of parliament was reported on October 29, 1990.

The spokesmen of [the National Council] asked the Patriarch of Moscow and All Russia not to perform the ritual in St. Sophia Cathedral but in any other church, since the Cathedral was a symbol of the state of Ukraine. The service in it is not a religious event, but a political one and we believe it to be nothing but a political provocation aimed against the state sovereignty of Ukraine. . . . We think such actions are a sign of the imperial policy of the Moscow Patriarchy that is joining forces with the central organs of the [Communist Party] in an attempt to save the last empire in the world. It is significant that the event took place at the time when the Patriarch of the Ukrainian Autocephalous Church, Mstyslav, is in the Ukraine and the Second Congress of Rukh is being held in Kiev. . . . [Chairman of Rukh, Ivan Drach, commented:] The fact that the Patriarch of Moscow and All Russia went into St. Sophia Cathedral through the back entrance brings shame to the Russian Orthodox Church. We will neither forget or forgive.[25]

The Ukrainian Autocephalous Orthodox versus the Ukrainian Catholics

The Ukrainian Autocephalous Orthodox church also represents a challenge to the Ukrainian Catholics, because at present it shows considerable strength almost entirely in Galicia, historically the stronghold of the Catholics. There is, in fact, evidence of considerable friction over the control of churches and the identity of parish priests as between the clergy and laity of the Catholics and the Autocephalous Orthodox.[26]

We have believers from the Ukrainian Catholic Church joining our Church. One example I can cite is the Horodenka [district] in Ivano-Frankivsk. . .where six, seven parishes went over to the UAOC. . . . At this time, we must understand that we are all Ukrainians and every Ukrainian has the right to join the Church of his choice; every person has the full right, and we cannot view this as some kind of tragedy because on our lands we find various confessions. . . . [A]ll churches can exist in Ukraine.

But Churches should also respect one another. If you want to form a Catholic church, be my guest, but it cannot be forced upon the people, as was the case in Stryi, that's in Lviv Oblast.

When the Catholics asked if we would give them one hour a day to serve their liturgy in a local church, we agreed, but within two weeks they took over the church, closed it and allowed it only for their own use. Similar incidents happened in Lviv, Ternopil, Ivano-Frankivsk. And finally, we began to forbid them the use of our churches. . . . We see such insincerity, such lack of brother-hood.[27]

A letter sent by Metropolitan Ioann and other Autocephalous Orthodox activists to leaders of Rukh and members of parliament further elaborates the same themes.

Our appeal is required by the strange activities of Catholic leaders, who acting in the name, and at the behest of Rukh, have gone be-yond the bounds of Christian principles. They have based their ac-tivities on hatred and hostility toward Orthodox Ukrainians. The aggression of Catholics, at first directed against the Russian Or-thodox Church, is now openly directed against the Autocephalous Church, which is defenseless. . . . It's becoming ever clearer that the whole campaign for the restoration of Catholicism, which at times is based even on violence, is an expression of group interests of people who have for a long time either openly or secretly been oriented toward Poland. One can pay attention to the strange coincidence between this campaign with the increasing activation of those circles in Poland who are proposing the return of Galicia under Polish rule. . . . This kind of division is being propagated by those "commissars" of Catholicism (we call them that because of the association that their personalities and methods evoke), who, taking the wish as the father to the thought, have become engaged in the second "Catholicization" of Galicia. The rebirth of Ukraine on the basis of [this kind of] spiritual subordination [has been]... thought up and obstinately forced on the people, and has no historical or moral justification. [It] is close to a betrayal of the Ukrainian idea, an idea which was always based on the freedom-loving Orthodox Cossaks, on the genius of the poet, Chevchen-cho, on the blue and yellow flag and the trident, which have nothing in common with Catholicism.... The Vatican and Catholicism never took the interests of Ukraine into account, or her strivings for independence.... The Vatican is supporting the recreation of "Little Poland" in Galicia.... The historical chance to revive a Ukrainian state is being used for the purposes of [instituting] a Catholic dictatorship and discrimination toward the Orthodox.... The organization of attacks on Ukrainian Orthodox churches, the categorization of the Orthodox as non-Ukrainians, as agents of the KGB, and the characterization of Orthodox rites and church acts as being invalid, such acts are directed to arouse hostility and to invoke opposition.... The struggle for human rights and in-dependence should not be identified with a struggle for the rule of Catholicism.[28]

For their part, Ukrainian Catholics believe they are being harassed and insulted by some priests and members of the Autocephalous church. The shortage of Catholic priests, as the result of persecu-tion, puts them at a distinct disadvantage in their attempt to reclaim and reactivate churches they hold to be theirs. They appeal for some consideration on the part of the Autocephalous in the allotment of churches while they undertake to train new clergy.[29] They reject claims that the Autocephalous church is the one genuinely nation-alist church because Orthodoxy is the only legitimate expression of Ukrainian religion. They also regard as ridiculous charges that they are Polish agents eager to restore Polish sovereignty over western Ukraine.

Finally, there is resentment among Ukrainian Catholics that, since liberalization, the Autocephalous have devoted more energy and attention to gaining control in western Ukraine than to reestablishing themselves in the east, where their traditional strength has been. There are recurring rumors, credited among many Ukrainian Catholics, that the Soviet government surreptitiously favors the Autocephalous church in redistributing churches in western Ukraine in order to dilute the radical independence movement that the Ukrainian Catholic church is taken to represent. Recently, a leader of the Ukrainian Catholic church complained that the appearance of the Autocephalous church in Catholic areas is "clearly a manipulation of the KGB."[30]

The Role of the Government

Finally, the divergent effects on the religious crisis of decisions at various levels of government must be emphasized.

The impact on the religious question of reasonably open democratic elections at the local and republican levels has been important. In spring and summer of 1990, the councils of deputies of the three provinces of Galicia in western Ukraine adopted resolutions declaring the act of liquidating the Ukrainian Catholic church at the Synod of Lviv to be null and void and calling for the return of all properties expropriated from the Catholics. At present, the determinations stand in a kind of limbo, for they were invalidated at the republican level of government and they have not been officially acknowledged or acted on at the central administrative level by the Council for Religious Affairs.

Still, there is momentum at the grass roots, and it will not be easy to quash. That is especially true because the democratic bloc now occupies somewhat less than one-third of the seats of the Ukrainian Supreme Soviet, and the same support for the Ukrainian Catholics exhibited in the local councils is now gathering strength at the republican level. There is talk of introducing resolutions akin to those adopted locally, which, by going farther than present legal proposals do, would have the effect of deciding the distribution of churches on the basis of a majority vote in each parish. It would simply bring to an end the entire leasing policy that now regulates the allocation of church property.[31]

On the other hand, these developments appear to conflict sharply with the policies of the central authorities, such as the Council for Religious Affairs. The council and other state authorities are firmly committed to the existing leasing law by which the Ukrainian branch of the Russian Orthodox church retains exclusive title to church property unless it decides voluntarily to surrender that title.

Much hangs, obviously, on which government prevails.

five

The Continuing Sources of Conflict

The Connection between
Religious and National Identity

In analyzing the sources of intolerance in Ukraine, the better to ameliorate them, it is important to consider whether the conflict is at bottom over national or religious identity.[1] Is the hostility basically the result of a belief in Ukrainian national independence and cultural autonomy that opposes Russia's own nationalistic designs on Ukraine? Is it, moreover, a conflict among Ukrainians as to who is truest to ethnic traditions? Or is the hostility better understood as fundamentally inspired by conflicting religious loyalties and beliefs among Ukrainian national churches on the one hand, and between them and Russian Orthodoxy on the other?

One answer is that "for many, many centuries, [the] national and ethnic identity of Ukrainians was determined by their religious identity. [But] now the situation is reversed completely. Now in most cases, not for peasants but for the nationally conscious Ukrainian intelligentsia, . . . religious identity is determined . . . by . . . national identity."[2]

Insofar as that is true, the essential problem is the nationality question. Once that question is resolved, religious differences may readily be overcome; this reversal might well be the product of the secularization process, the process of transforming religious consciousness into something with a more this-worldly reference, namely, national or ethnic consciousness (p. 11).

However, there are reasons to think that the connection between religious and national identity in Ukraine is more complicated. For one, this account itself admits that religion is more salient for the peasants than for the intelligentsia, suggesting that the priority of national over religious identity may vary from group to group. What is more, the account also concedes that under existing circumstances strictly religious conflicts may likely "divert attention... from... purely political issues" and may therefore be "considered more dangerous" to the cause of peace "than the question of... purely ethnic identity."[3] If religion is capable of producing such an effect, then it must be assumed to have some continuing motivational efficacy.

But there are additional considerations peculiar to Ukraine that make it particularly difficult to disentangle religious from national identity[4] and thus to settle conclusively the question of causal priority.

The first complication concerns the interdependence of beliefs about religion and national origins. In a fundamental sense, the three-way dispute among the Russian (renamed Ukrainian)[5] Orthodox, the Ukrainian Autocephalous Orthodox, and the Ukrainian Catholics turns on ethnic issues. The names of the groups themselves illustrate that fact. The charges and counter-charges invariably get back to questions of national loyalty. A key disagreement between the Autocephalous Orthodox and the Russian Orthodox concerns whether the Kievan Rus', the normative tenth-century community, was Russian or Ukrainian in character and therefore whether the Orthodoxy introduced in 988 was Russian or non-Russian. Similarly, a key disagreement between the

Ukrainiàn Catholics on the one side and both Orthodox churches on the other is whether the geographical and ethnic division between Western and Eastern Christianity in the eleventh century, after the formation of Kievan religion, was aberrant and unnatural (as the Catholics believe) or required and justified (as the Orthodox believe).

A second complication is that the Soviet state, informed first by Marxism-Leninism and then by Stalin's version of Communist-Russian imperialism, itself politicized religion, making a sharp distinction between state and church impossible. The particular events that, in recent experience, decisively shaped the life and self-understanding of the Ukrainian national churches illustrate that fact. The Ukrainian Catholic church, after all, was liquidated in 1946 by an act of state, an act that not only expropriated all church property but also subjected the church to a government-initiated policy of systematic discrimination and persecution. Essentially the same fate befell the Autocephalous Orthodox church as the result of a government decision in 1930 to dissolve the church. What was regarded by the Soviet government as unorthodox belief on the part of the national churches was anathematized as politically dangerous and potentially seditious.

Beyond that, Stalin, in particular, came to define religion in nationalistic terms. To engage the Russian Orthodox church as an instrument for extending and consolidating centralized political control over territories like Ukraine was to structure things in such a way that religious resistance by the national churches was inevitably interpreted ''as a demand for a separate [national] identity, or at least for the strengthening of a national sense of identity.''[6]

If Russian Orthodoxy is seen as ''the imperial church which integrates Ukrainians, Belorussians, Moldavians with Russians,'' the Ukrainian Catholic church is ''perceived as a separatist church, because it breaks up empire.''[7] The same would be true of the Ukrainian Autocephalous Orthodox church. Faced with circumstances of that sort, religious believers, whether they like it or not, would be compelled to understand their outlawed beliefs, practices, and forms of church organization as having a political consequence of the profoundest kind.[8]

These observations extend to the sensitive sociological question of trying to identify exactly who religious believers are and how they conceive of themselves in the Ukrainian context.[9] Because the national churches were legally prohibited, overt religious identification, especially for the Catholics and the Autocephalous, was a severe liability until very recently. Consequently, to expect deeply entrenched and highly elaborate patterns of religious identification would be unreasonable.[10] In addition, there is the question of "who is a secret believer, who is not a believer, who claims to be Orthodox, but is really a Ukrainian Catholic, who claims to be a Communist, but secretly is a believer; it has become a Pandora's Box. It is only now that these things are being sorted out. . ."(p. 8).

Although religious differences do exist, they are at present most acutely defined in reference to what is essentially *a political and legal problem:* the conflict over the possession and occupancy of state-expropriated church property. To repeat: Because of the historical context, the question of religious identity is inextricably intertwined with political and nationalist considerations.

The same interpretation applies, again, to the fact that religious identity in Ukraine, particularly among the members of the national churches, does not include a very developed consciousness of tradition and doctrine but tends to be reduced to a rather primitive form of group loyalty. "[D]eplorable incidents [occurring] mostly on the parish level. . .are often initiated by priests who pursue their own egoistic goals. Villagers are not infrequently involved in conflicts not because they share confessional prejudices but because they follow their priests."[11]

The main cause of this situation is that all opportunity for religious education and training has been systematically suppressed by the government. "The Ukrainian Catholic Church has been deprived of any theological institutions and publications for forty-five years. The people who have completed formal theological education are in their seventies."[12] Although the monastic orders, operating clandestinely, have succeeded in training some new clergy and in keeping awareness of church traditions alive to some degree, they have, of course, operated against great odds.[13] It remains to be seen what the effects of the relaxation of restrictions on religious education and publication will be for upgrading religious self-understanding.

Finally, even recent examples of voting behavior reflecting religious interests cannot, it appears, be understood apart from the political-historical context. That support for the legalization of Ukrainian Catholics contributed to the success of the democratic bloc in western Ukraine is surely not the result of purely religious considerations. Favoring the Ukrainian Catholic church is one important way of making a strongly political statement under present circumstances. It expresses the repudiation of policies associated with Soviet domination, thereby indicating support for independent national identity (p. 8).

Memory and Justice: The Question of Restitution

The interconnection of religious and national identity makes solving the problem of religious intolerance difficult without considering the political context, including the nationalistic impulses that are so much a part of the picture. This difficulty applies particularly to the burning issue of rectification for past injustices.[14]

In cases of religious and related forms of intolerance, conflict is typically fueled by irreconcilable accounts or stories of historical grievances. Ukrainian Catholics perceive themselves to be the aggrieved victims of an act of infamy—the Synod of Lviv. The occasion by which Catholics were robbed of their rights and means of worship and subjected to discrimination and persecution is remembered as an event with inseparable political and religious significance. It was perpetrated, according to the Catholic account, by two culprits working in complicity with each other, the Soviet state and the Russian Orthodox church.

Therefore, the key to reconciliation and peace is, from the Catholic point of view, a thorough admission of wrongdoing and an acceptance of responsibility for it on the part of *both* church and state, entailing a formal declaration of the illegitimacy of the Synod of Lviv and a commitment to the immediate return of all properties confiscated from the church. The repudiation or serious qualification of charges of collaboration with the Nazis during World War II is, of course, intended to correct the historical record by discrediting any allegations of guilt that might be used to try to justify the decisions taken at the Synod of Lviv.

The Russian Orthodox story—at least the hierarchy's official story—is sharply divergent. Because Ukrainian Catholicism was illegitimate and artificially imposed to begin with, the Synod of Lviv violated no one's rights. Stalin's acts of persecution were not condoned, but there was no cause to object to the outlawing of the church. In fact, the result was beneficial in that it properly overturned what was widely agreed to have been an "unnatural union" with Rome, something that was "a source of national, social and religious oppression."[15] It is emphasized, in addition, that the Russian Orthodox have been faithful stewards of the churches entrusted to them by the state and, as such, they have earned the right to special consideration in the distribution of church property.

Even on this account, there might be room for compensating violations committed by Stalin and subsequent Soviet regimes that deprived individual believers of ordinary civil protections. But there would be no grounds for returning church property, because the church as an institution had no validity and therefore has no rightful claim.

So long as believers on either side of the conflict adhere staunchly to these contradictory stories, there is little prospect that the churches can, on their own initiative, settle their differences and reduce the level of intolerance. There are, of course, certain indications that the dissidents or independent thinkers in the Russian Orthodox church represent a measure of flexibility and a willingness to reconsider the credibility of the official story and possibly to begin the difficult task of restructuring the church's collective memory.

Some observers contend that such concessions are essential for the cause of peace, especially from the Russian Orthodox side.[16]

> I think it is important that the mistakes made in the past should come out. . . . [W]e cannot build a future without a full and complete acknowledgement and revelation and declaration [of] what happened in the past. . . . There has been external perestroika [so far as the Russian Church has readjusted to a new political and social environment]. [B]ut there hasn't been internal perestroika, no fresh initiative [at least not, so far, from the hierarchy].[17]

> If we have Russians who are willing to say that Lvov was a fraud and that the Ukrainian Catholics were not guilty of collaboration with the Nazis, that says something about the possibilities of progress in the direction of [observing] international standards. On the other hand, if the standard histories with their obvious accusatory and apologetic purposes are still believed by many Russians, there seems less possibility of an accord between the Russian Orthodox and the Ukrainian Catholics. At the popular level, such histories may remain a powerful and dangerous source of animosity between members of these churches.[18]

But however important it may be that concessions of the recommended sort be made in the interests of peace and justice, and however forthcoming certain segments of the Russian Orthodox church are, the revision of collective memory is a painful and difficult task, not easily susceptible to external pressures of one kind or another. It can only be urged and invited. Whereas public confession of wrongdoing may perhaps be compelled, "repentance cannot be. . . . The voluntary movement toward repentance occurring in some circles in religion is likely in the long-term to be more fruitful and more healing than enforced confession from the leaders of the church might be. . . . If you force a confession from people, you may not get what you're actually aiming for, which is the alleviation of intolerance. [You simply] push. . .people into a corner."[19]

If the churches, and especially the Russian Orthodox church, have difficulty revising their story, the central government has already gone some distance in that regard. The regional and local branches of government in the Ukraine have, of course, gone even farther. The implications for peace of the various changes in the government's interpretation of the past are important.

So far as the central authorities go, there is little equivocating over a general evaluation, at least, of the Synod of Lviv. "Of course it was unjust, and dictated from above. . . ."[20] In one utterance, there is acknowledgment and confirmation by the Council for Religious Affairs of some of the central convictions of the Ukrainian Catholics: the synod was illegitimate, and it produced abuses against the Catholics. The government has taken steps to rectify the injustice by legalizing the church, releasing prisoners of conscience, permitting religious liberty to an unprecedented degree, and so on.

Still, the authorities do not go so far as to embrace all the basic demands of the Catholics. They have in fact invalidated resolutions adopted by the Council of Deputies strongly condemning the Synod of Lviv and nullifying the liquidation of the Ukrainian Catholic church. Furthermore, it is admitted that, far from restoring confiscated Catholic property, the present leasing law—which the government supports and which accords exclusive legal control over disputed church property to the Orthodox—exhibits, if not a clear legal privilege, a distinct "predisposition" in favor of the Russian Orthodox.[21] That means, of course, that in the dispute between the Catholics and the Russian Orthodox, the interests of the latter are, in effect, preferred.

Indeed, by providing an historical account that supports the leasing law as it stands, the government's collective memory of events is, in the end, also predisposed toward the Russian church. In 1946, "nobody took the churches as such . . . away from the people. . . . The churches remained and the parishes remained, only from a certain date [the people] were told you are not Greek Catholic any longer, you are Orthodox. But they were able to come to the same churches and to practice their religion."[22]

So far as the question of the occupancy of churches goes, the injustice visited on the Ukrainian Catholics was, it is claimed by Kolesnyk, rather insignificant. To be sure, they were prevented from identifying themselves publicly as Catholics. Otherwise, however, "they were able to come to the *same churches and to practice their religion*" (emphasis added). Considered just as a religious issue, the matter has been seriously exaggerated (p. 17). There is no cause for hostility of the sort that has broken out around western Ukraine, nor for extravagant talk about the need for public acts of expiation and restitution.

To the extent that there is a valid dispute between the two parties, it should be subject to manageable mediation and resolution, once the irrationality or the emotional affect that has attached itself to this matter has been dispelled. For the central government, the way to peace is to recover balance and a sense of proportion by means of a more dispassionate recollection of what actually happened in 1946.

Such an interpretation seems only a slight modification of the official Russian Orthodox version. The unmistakable implication is that the law, which, in effect, supports the claims of the Russian Orthodox, is essentially a good and reasonable law. From the Ukrainian Catholic perspective, far from confessing its guilt and restructuring its memory in this matter, the government appears simply to perpetuate the legacy of intolerance by reaffirming in qualified but finally uncompromising tones the traditional alliance between the central government and the Russian Orthodox church. This attitude is, it appears, generally consistent with the government's practical policy in regard to leasing churches previously under the control of Ukrainian Catholics. It is still not official policy to extend formal registration to any Ukrainian Catholic church.

But whatever the predisposition of the central authorities, events have, to a degree, overtaken them. Local councils of deputies and state authorities are in many cases taking things into their own hands and making decisions concerning the disposition of church property that disregard the leasing policy conventionally applied by the central government. Of course, whether this procedure, which effectively bypasses the established centrally controlled political and legal mechanisms, will eventually bring peace, justice, and reconciliation among the warring churches remains to be seen.

There are, it seems, sensitive and complex questions concerning what is fair and proper so far as restoring confiscated property is concerned. For one thing, existing human rights norms ''don't give us much guidance about how to resolve competing claims'' for restitution.[23] Certainly, the Declaration against Intolerance does not contain any provisions for resolving problems of this sort. It appears that more attention ought to be given to this matter in the development of human rights theory.

For another thing, it may not, as a matter of justice, be acceptable to ignore completely Russian Orthodox claims concerning their property rights in the disputes with the Catholics and Autocephalous Orthodox. ''Might there not be a claim of justice on the part of some Russian Orthodox congregations. . .to have [a] particular church, even though the original set of factors which led to [their] taking over the church were illegitimate? Might it not be possible, depending on your theory of justice, to have a rightful claim to a church even though the 1946 Synod was illegitimate?''[24]

An argument to that effect might be premised on the belief that forty years of faithful administration in the forced absence of the rightful owner entitles the caretaker to special consideration in the final disposition of the property and, perhaps, to some share of the final allocation. On that construction, both the Catholics and the Russian Orthodox might register legitimate claims. Even so, it would, of course, remain to be seen exactly how those claims were to be adjudicated.

However, such an argument requires that both parties agree in the first place on the identity of the ''rightful owner'' and the ''caretaker.'' But that, it seems, is what much of the dispute is in fact about. The comments made by the Russian Orthodox hierarchy questioning the very legitimacy of the Ukrainian Catholics[25] clearly challenge the Catholic church's right to ownership and imply that the church property in question rightfully belonged to the Russian Orthodox church to begin with. Until agreement is achieved concerning the legitimacy of the parties to the dispute, the prospects for harmoniously resolving the problem of restitution seem dim.

Conciliation Attempts

Several efforts have been mounted since the beginning of 1990 to resolve the conflict between the Ukrainian Catholics and the Russian Orthodox by means of official discussion and negotiation. However, to date none of these efforts has given much basis for hope. Delegations of the Vatican and the Russian Orthodox church met in Moscow on January 12 through 17, 1990, and agreed to recommendations regarding the normalization of relations between the two churches in Western Ukraine. The Ukrainian Catholics were disappointed in these recommendations, which neither recommended the full recognition of the Catholic church nor advocated acknowledging its existence and authority. More constructively, parties agreed to create the joint Quadripartite Commission for administering the process of normalization between the two churches. The commission was to include one or two representatives each from the Vatican, the Moscow patriarchate, the western Ukraine Orthodox, and the Ukrainian Catholics. Regarded as especially urgent were the disputes over church property.[26]

The first meeting of the Quadripartite Commission took place in Kiev on March 6. According to one of the Ukrainian Catholic delegates, Archbishop Volodymyr Sterniuk of Lviv,

> the delegation of the Moscow Patriarchate quickly took control of the commission's agenda and skillfully manipulated the proceedings as well as the subsequent visit to Galicia to isolate and alienate the two Uniate representatives from Western Ukraine. On March 13, Sterniuk walked out from the Quadripartite Commission's meeting in protest against, above all, the Moscow Patriarchate's refusal to concede the invalidity of the 1946 "Lviv Sobor" and to recognize the canonical, corporate nature of the Greek Catholic Church and its hierarchy. The walkout of the Greek Catholic representatives from the Commission and their list of fourteen demands which the latter refused to consider, were on March 17 endorsed by the remaining Uniate bishops in Galicia.[27]

After the breakdown of the March meeting, relations between the two churches worsened. There were increasing conflicts over local churches. The Moscow patriarchate stepped up its criticism of the Ukrainian Catholics and formed a committee for the defense of the rights of the Orthodox church.

A second meeting of the commission convened in Moscow on September 14 again ended abruptly. No final statement was adopted. "The talks were not fruitful for the Orthodox side," Metropolitan Filaret reported.[28] The Greek-Catholic representatives from Lviv and Ivano-Frankivsk refused to comply with the Orthodox request that they be given the Church of the Transfiguration and the palace chapel of the St. George Cathedral in Lviv, and the Holy Resurrection Cathedral in Ivano-Frankivsk. The Russian Orthodox representatives contended they were being arbitrarily deprived of the bishops' cathedrals in western Ukraine that rightfully belonged to them.

Archbishop Sterniuk of the Ukrainian Catholic church responded "that there are few parishes in Western Ukraine attached to the Moscow Patriarchate because this was the will of the faithful. The archbishop said that under these circumstances, the Orthodox requests were impossible to consider. . . . After some time, [the Orthodox] broke off the talks stating that it was impossible to hold discussions with the Catholics."[29]

As to the prospect for discussions between the Russian Orthodox and the Autocephalous Orthodox, the outlook is equally gloomy. Metropolitan Ioann of the Autocephalous church makes clear that there is nothing to discuss. "We will ask [the Russian Orthodox hierarchy] to leave the Ukrainian lands. We have no room for them. They have often said Ukraine does not exist, it never has, it never will. They have never [preached] a sermon to the people in the Ukrainian language. They hate everything Ukrainian. The Ukrainian people do not need them; others we will welcome into the ranks of the [Autocephalous] Church."[30]

As yet, there have been no formal attempts at conciliation between the Ukrainian Catholics and the Autocephalous Orthodox, although there are expressions of hope that "a common language" between the two churches can be discovered despite continuing difficulties.[31] Metropolitan Mstyslav of the Autocephalous church believes that cooperation between the two churches, which has existed in the past, is possible in the future if external elements with their own mischievous interests can be prevented from further meddling in church affairs.[32]

six

Conclusion

In one sense, the Ukrainian case presents a ringing vindication of the Declaration against Intolerance. It is now publicly and officially admitted by representatives of the Soviet government, and widely confirmed by the testimony of the Soviet people, that the seventy-year campaign conducted in the name of Marxism-Leninism and extended and adapted by Stalin—a campaign that suppressed, dominated, and manipulated religion by means of systematic discrimination and persecution—was a colossal failure and a cause for shame.

The recent adoption of the new Law on Freedom of Conscience and Religion symbolizes the total repudiation of policies of intolerance toward expressing and practicing religious and other beliefs that have, as the declaration puts it, ''brought great suffering'' to the citizens of the Soviet Union, as well as ''kindl[ed] hatred between peoples'' who make up the Soviet state. Article 4 of the new law recalls the declaration: ''Any direct or indirect limitation on the rights of a citizen or the establishment of any advantages for citizens depending on their attitude towards religion, and equally incitement of enmity or hostility associated with this, or insult against the sentiments of citizens, are subject to criminal liability as established by law.''

Furthermore, Ukrainian local legislators, together with Rukh (the Ukrainian People's Movement for Perestroika) are publicly committed to a thoroughgoing respect for freedom of conscience and religious pluralism and to beginning the task of disengaging the state from exclusive identity with one religion in preference to others.[1] Finally, there are occasionally firm, if highly general, expressions of commitment to pluralism and religious liberty by officials of the three disputing churches. Leaders of each church appear to assume, at least in theory, that a system of tolerance of the sort outlined in the declaration is the best means of achieving lasting and just peace in Ukraine.

Still, theory is one thing, practice another. The abiding difficulty in Ukraine is how to implement a system of tolerance, how to restructure attitudes and behavior patterns so as to bring them into conformity with the declaration. That task requires no less than a revolution in the ways of thinking and acting that have become entrenched by long-standing historical outlook and experience, by what we have referred to as the legacy of intolerance. Clearly, the revolution has already begun and even now is profoundly affecting legal and political as well as religious conditions in the country. There is significant movement toward a new, more tolerant Ukraine.

But two specific and interrelated problem areas of major importance remain. The future role of the central Soviet government in Ukraine will need to be examined in reference to the imperatives of the declaration. To the extent that the existing leasing law, which favors the Russian Orthodox church and which is in no way affected by the new law on freedom of religion, actually continues to determine the disposition of church property in Ukraine, the law may have a discriminatory effect and thus stand in conflict with article 2 of the declaration.[2] Not only is the leasing law admittedly predisposed toward the interests of the Russian Orthodox church,[3] it also legalizes what government representatives now agree was the unjust transfer of Ukrainian Catholic church property into Orthodox hands in 1946.[4] Of course, if the law becomes irrelevant because of new political and legislative developments in Ukraine, this issue will lose its significance.

Probably more important is the question of the central government's alleged covert role in encouraging the expansion of the Autocephalous church in western Ukraine. It is widely claimed that the central government is surreptitiously supporting the Autocephalous in their efforts to gain control over churches the Catholics consider rightfully theirs. There are also allegations that the government is helping to foment further strife and bad feeling between the churches. The supposed object is to inhibit Catholic growth in Galicia and Transcarpathia and thereby to frustrate the radical independence movement the Catholics are believed to represent. If this claim is true—and it is, to be sure, hard to verify— then such action would appear to be highly discriminatory and clearly contrary to the declaration.

Second, entrenched and pervasive thoughts about the relation of religious to civil and national identity need to be modified. According to the declaration, civil legitimacy and religious legitimacy are *separate questions.* A group's or an individual's civil rights to equal treatment, freedom of expression, and so on do not depend on demonstrated conformity to a prescribed set of religious or other basic beliefs. From a religious point of view, one church or religious group may well judge the beliefs and practices of another group to lack authority and to be in serious error. Such a judgment, however, in no way detracts from the right of that group to express and practice its religion as it sees fit and to enjoy equally all the civil privileges and opportunities available to the first group.

Yet, because of the history of the region and particularly the religious life and outlook, issues of spiritual legitimacy and civil or national legitimacy are deeply intertwined. The idea of the imperial church, historically identified with Russian Orthodoxy, exemplifies the interconnection dramatically. That idea, among other things, disposed the Orthodox church to accommodate itself to Stalin's brand of Russian nationalism and, accordingly, to support and defend the liquidation of the Ukrainian national churches. To be spiritually illegitimate is at the same time to be civilly and nationally unworthy. Even in the flush of glasnost and perestroika, that view continues to be expressed by the Russian Orthodox hierarchy, severely impairing the spread of the doctrine of religious liberty.

But there is evidence that some leaders and members of the national churches hold a similar view. To contend, as does Metropolitan Ioann of the Autocephalous church, that "there never was a Greek Catholic Church historically," that it was "forcibly established" as a product of Polish domination, and that "Ukrainianism was preserved better [by Ukrainian] Orthodoxy" is to interconnect, rather than separate, issues of religious and national identity.[5] It is to cast aspersions on the national and civic loyalty of a group and to raise questions about their status as citizens because they hold religious convictions that are regarded as mistaken. In short, it perpetuates the belief that, so far as authentic citizenship goes, one religious group is to be preferred over others.

In contrast to such views, one scholar puts forward the following model for religious and national life in Ukraine, which appears to reflect the spirit of the declaration:

> Th[e] model involves the withdrawal of the party and the state from civil society, or at least separation [from them]. The state should have nothing to do with the churches as churches. Any laws should be laws that pertain to all citizens, not just the believers. There should be no dominance [or] subordinate relationship between the nationalities. . . . Either [a] very loose union or non-union in which nationalities, [and all affected] religions, are equal and have self-expression, politically, culturally, socially, otherwise, and the kind of neutral state that does not determine which [religion] is the favorite daughter. . . . In other words, [it would be] the kind of pluralistic civil society. . . in which the state [separates itself] from the realm of conscience. That is really the model which seems to be inspiring democratic movements, whatever future awaits them in the Soviet Union. But once this type of relationship between nationality and religious policy. . .

takes root, becomes a reality, then this other wrapping, this intert-
wining, this overshadowing of religion by nationalism. . .will very
much dissipate. [R]eligious tolerance, inter-religious dialogue, and
freedom to choose between a religion, among religions and between religion and whatever you would call it, agnosticism or
non-belief, will become possible. It is still not possible.[6]

In light of the comments about nationality policy, it ought to be
emphasized that the declaration also appears to imply that just as
individuals may not be civilly disadvantaged or treated unequally
for their religious beliefs, so they may not be disadvantaged or
treated unequally for holding and expressing certain ethnic or national beliefs—certain beliefs, that is, about the origins, basic warrants, and proper character of one's nation. Under the declaration,
divergent national stories, involving as they do basic beliefs about
the foundations of national legitimacy, seem to be as protected, as
subject to the conditions of tolerance, as are divergent religious
stories. No doubt it is because beliefs about national legitimacy are
so fundamental that they frequently overlap or intermingle with
religious beliefs. Similar protection for both sets of beliefs therefore
seems perfectly consistent.

The model of the separation of church and state and of religious
pluralism and tolerance so widely and enthusiastically advocated
these days throughout Ukraine no doubt faces substantial impedi-
ments. There is the problem of disentangling religion and politics
in settings such as Ukraine, where people are long predisposed to
interconnect them. It may prove very difficult to transpose Western
models, developed as the result of unique circumstances, into un-
familiar surroundings.[7] It is, moreover, an open question whether
Western models are actually working as well as they used to and
whether those models can successfully accommodate the revolutionary and conflicting forces that are emerging with new vigor in
various parts of the world.[8]

On the other hand, however difficult the task of overcoming the
legacy of intolerance in Ukraine may be, consideration of the causes
and effects of that legacy appears to underscore for a significant

number of Ukrainians the relevance and power of the model of pluralism and religious liberty elaborated in a document such as the UN Declaration against Intolerance. The new devotion to the basic ideas of that document, repeatedly enunciated in public statements by Ukrainian observers as well as by local political officials and by the leaders of Rukh, has been born of long and bitter experience with the effects of politicized religion. "Excessive Church involvement in state affairs carries dangers of abuse, such as lay control of the Church for political purposes. It is questionable whether a state Church would really benefit from its privileged status in spiritual terms. The fate of the Russian Orthodox Church should be a warning in this regard."[9]

Because of the unstable and uncertain state of affairs in the Soviet Union in general and Ukraine in particular, it is impossible to predict the outcome of present efforts at restructuring. Because a necessary condition for pluralism and tolerance in Ukraine is a radical redefinition of the role of the central government in Ukrainian affairs, the recent drift toward a policy of crackdown in the republics underscores the fragility of new developments.

Nevertheless, whichever arrangement eventually emerges, Ukrainian history has already confirmed unmistakably the essential message of the Declaration against Intolerance. A system in which the conscience is free, one that effectively prohibits intolerance and discrimination based on religion or belief by differentiating the religious from the civil order, is a critical part of the struggle for peace, social justice, and friendship among people.

Afterword

According to information received at the end of 1990,[1] several significant developments have occurred that are relevant to the foregoing account. First, except for a few scattered parishes, the conflict in western Ukraine between the national churches and the Russian Orthodox church (now called Ukrainian Orthodox) is declining in importance. Most of the priests who served for so long as Russian Orthodox have elected to join either the Ukrainian Catholic church or the Ukrainian Autocephalous Orthodox church. Although numerous Russian (Ukrainian) Orthodox parishes remain in the eastern part of Ukraine, where most people of Russian extraction reside, very few such parishes exist now in the west.[2]

Second, the leasing arrangements, which ascribed to the Russian Orthodox church rights of occupancy over church property and which therefore produced considerable conflict between the Russian Orthodox and the national churches, have increasingly been ignored. Distribution of church property has been worked out locally on the basis of new contracts drawn up between the district government and the churches. These new contracts favor the national churches because, as it is asserted, so few clergy and members have remained in the Russian (Ukrainian) Orthodox church. This development means that the conflicts over church property between the Russian Orthodox and the national churches have also been subsiding.

Third, the focus of church strife in the west is now squarely between the Ukrainian Catholics and the Autocephalous Orthodox. Although there are few instances of overt violence, considerable hatred and anger toward one another are manifest. The issue between the two groups is no longer so much over church occupancy, although some tension does continue even there. Local decisions have moderated the disputes over possession, and the Catholics have modified their demand that they receive full restitution for confiscated property.[3] Nevertheless, proposals by Catholics that church buildings be shared in situations of divided affiliation have frequently been rejected by the Autocephalous hierarchy.

Nor is the tension particularly generated by religious or confessional differences. The conflict at bottom is over ''patriotism and [national] self-identity,'' over ''what it means to be Ukrainian.''

> What's driving the conflict is the intensity of both peoples' desire for what they perceive to be an independent Ukraine, for what it should be like. . . . The Catholics consider the Autocephalous to be basically Moscow-controlled, or at least somehow connected, or tainted, to be KGB-infiltrated. . . . The Autocephalous faithful consider the Ukrainian Catholic Church to be a Polish church, allied to a Polish Pope, [with] their loyalties. . . elsewhere, not really with Ukraine. The Autocephalous consider themselves to be the true Ukrainian church, the church of the Cossacks, and the bearers of that heritage.[4]

Fourth, it is widely alleged that the Soviet central government and the Russian Orthodox hierarchy continue to play a role in fueling the hostility between the two national churches.[5]

Fifth, the elimination of intolerance depends on creating an effective legal and political system ''based on Western standards. . . . There will be absolutely no favoritism of one church or confession over another. The model here is the Western idea of religious tolerance and religious pluralism.''[6] The system will, however, need to be worked out by the Ukrainians themselves. The Soviet law on freedom of conscience, although a step in the right direction, is by now essentially irrelevant to the Ukrainian situation. A new Ukrainian constitution is in process of being drafted, and it will include stringent provisions for the protection of religious freedom.[7]

Notes

"About the Series"

1. Angelo Vidal d'Almeida Ribeiro, *Implementation of the Declaration on the Elimination of All Forms of Intolerance and of Discrimination Based on Religion or Belief*, report to the UN Commission on Human Rights, E/CN.4/1990/46, p. 58. "This background leads us to a brief reflection on the grim reality that the problem of intolerance and discrimination based on religion or belief is one of great magnitude today despite the existence of far-reaching guarantees of the right to freedom of thought, conscience, religion and belief in the constitutions of many states, of provisions to prevent and punish interference with legitimate manifestations of religions or beliefs in the laws and regulations of those States, and of continuing efforts on the part of Governments, religions, and beliefs, to foster tolerance by means of education. The problem involves not only discrimination negating rights and freedoms of individuals and groups of different religions and beliefs, but also attitudes and manifestations of intolerance between religions and beliefs, between individuals and groups having different religions and beliefs, as well as between nations and within nations" (Elizabeth Odio Benito, *Study of the Current Dimensions of the Problems of Intolerance and of Discrimination on Grounds of Religion or Belief*, UN Doc. E/CN.4/Sub.2/1987/26, p. 26).

2. d'Almeida Ribeiro, *Implementation of the Declaration*, p. 59.

3. Benito, *Study of Current Dimensions*, p. 39.

4. "As a result of lengthy discussions in various international bodies, it is now generally accepted that 'religion or belief' includes theistic, non-theistic, and atheistic belief" (ibid., p. 3).

5. See Donna Sullivan, "Advancing the Freedom of Religion or Belief through the UN Declaration on the Elimination of Religious Intolerance and Discrimination," *American Journal of International Law*, 82 (1988): 504–506.

6. Sullivan, "Advancing Freedom of Religion," p. 505. "It has been realized that intolerance based on religion or belief has two separate aspects: first, an unfavorable attitude of mind towards persons or groups of a different religion or belief, and secondly, manifestations of such an attitude in practice. Such manifestations often take the form of discrimination, but in many cases they go much further and involve the stirring up of hatred against, or even the persecution of, individuals or groups of a different religion or belief" (Benito, *Study of Current Dimensions*, p. 3).

7. See for example, Nat Hentoff, "Stanford and the Speech Police," *Washington Post*, July 7, 1990, in which a recent policy against "discriminatory harassment" at Stanford University is criticized. This policy raises precisely the issue of perplexities concerning the proper limits of free speech. "A Stanford student is forbidden to use 'speech or other expression' that is 'intended to [directly] insult or stigmatize an individual or a small number of individuals on the basis of their sex, race, color, handicap, religion, sexual orientation or national and ethnic origin.'" Excluded are "fighting words"—words whose "very utterance inflict injury or tend to incite to an immediate breach of peace"—uttered against minorities. The regulation is interpreted not to protect the white majority from slanderous speech or gestures. Hentoff argues that such a regulation is hopelessly slippery. "Will a Stanford student suffer greater punishment for insulting an Italian-American in contrast to saying awful things to a Presbyterian?" He asserts that, by adopting such a policy, Stanford "has turned foolish and has forgotten why it and other colleges exist. Suppression of speech is not the reason, or it didn't use to be."

8. So long as we remember what we are doing, the convenience of using one word—intolerance—to cover both attitudes and practices as a kind of shorthand is considerable and fully in line with ordinary usage. In common speech, patterns of religious discrimination and persecution provide evidence for the existence of intolerance. That is true, no doubt, because, as the preceding discussion points out, to discriminate against or to persecute an individual or a group appears to be one important way of giving expression to intolerance. For analytical purposes, it is still open, of course, to specify the more refined meaning of intolerance (in regard specifically to attitudes) where such distinctions are important.

9. James Madison substituted "the concept of freedom of conscience for the . . . idea of toleration. The difference was dramatically stated by Thomas Paine: 'Toleration is not the opposite of intolerance, but it is the counterfeit of it. Both are despotisms. The one assumes to itself the right of withholding liberty of conscience, the other of granting it. The one is the pope armed with fire and faggot, the other is the pope selling or granting indulgences'" (Robert L. Ketchum, "James Madison and Religion: A New Hypothesis," in *James Madison on Religious Liberty*, edited by Robert S. Alley [Buffalo, N.Y.: Prometheus Books, 1985], pp. 187–88).

10. See D. W. Hamlyn, *The Theory of Knowledge* (Garden City, N.Y.: Doubleday & Co., 1970), pp. 86–95.

11. Niccolo Machiavelli, *The Prince and the Discourses* (New York: Modern Library, 1950), pp. 65–66.

12. Max Weber, "The Meaning of Discipline," in *From Max Weber: Essays in Sociology*, edited by H. H. Gerth and C. Wright Mills (New York: Oxford University Press, 1958), p. 262.

13. Sullivan, "Advancing Freedom of Religion," pp. 492ff.

14. If a convincing case can be made that the public expression of a belief constitutes a direct incitement to rebellion, then that is usually considered a justified reason for punishing or suppressing the public expression of that belief. The difficulties arise when a government is suspected of using its accepted authority to suppress sedition as a pretext for suppressing unseditious criticism.

1. "Introduction to Ukraine"

1. The name *Ukraine* comes from the word meaning *borderland*. Because Russians regard the Ukrainian Republic as the borderland of the Russian Republic, they typically employ the definite article in referring to it; hence, "the Ukraine." That usage is most familiar to non-Soviets. By contrast, Ukrainians tend to drop the definite article, implying that the republic stands by itself and is not anybody else's borderland. Because a decision between the uses must be made, the Ukrainian usage without the definite article has been adopted in this study.

2. The following comments are either summaries or direct quotations from Kolesnyk, "Restructuring the State-to-Church Relationship, and Paths toward the Normalization of the Religious Situation in Ukraine," paper presented to the working group conference (translation from the Russian text), pp. 3–4, or from his remarks during the discussion.

3. Bohdan R. Bociurkiw, "The Politics of Religion in Ukraine under Gorbachev: The Case of the Ukrainian Catholic Church," paper presented to the working group conference, p. 3. Cf. Father Frank Estocin, "Summary of Remarks Concerning the Ukrainian Autocephalous Orthodox Church," paper presented to the working group conference, p. 1.

4. Bociurkiw, "Politics of Religion in Ukraine," p. 3.

5. Kolesnyk: "I do not feel and I cannot say that there is any deep felt or expressed anti-Semitism now in Ukraine. . . . Of course there are lots of unresolved problems of the Soviet Jewish population. . . . But as far as the attitude of the Ukrainian government is concerned, they are totally against any exhibition or display of anti-Semitism, and . . . as far as in their power, they will not tolerate anything done in this direction" (transcript of the working group conference, vol. 1 [hereafter, transcript, vol. 1], p. 22). Kolesnyk's comments were confirmed by Orest Vlokh, a regional leader of Rukh (Ukrainian People's Movement for Perestroika) and recently elected member of the Ukrainian Parliament, who was present in the audience. Kolesnyk's remarks were also confirmed by Jaroslav Isayevych in his written response to Father Estocin's paper: "All objective observers agree that the Ukraine nowadays has no anti-Semitic movement" (p. 5). On the other hand, see David S. Broder, "Hope and Danger in the Ukraine," *Washington Post*, July 22, 1990: "[In Ukraine the] Jewish question is a particularly sensitive one for Rukh leaders, given the area's history of anti-Jewish pogroms. Mykhailo Horyn stressed to me that Rukh had several Jews in its leadership, was establishing three Jewish cultural centers in Kiev, had issued three statements decrying anti-Semitism and had sent a prominent Jewish psychiatrist from Kiev as its first unofficial 'envoy' to the West. But a Ukrainian geography teacher I met while doing random on-the-street interviews in Moscow said that while he admired Rukh's ideals, 'I fear the people who have come under its banner.' Since Rukh came to power in his home city, he said, anti-Semitic slogans have been scrawled on the walls of the elevator in his apartment building, 'and my children for the first time are afraid.'" Such fears have been credited by *Washington Jewish Week*. That newspaper has portrayed Rukh as an anti-Semitic organization (see report in *The Ukrainian Weekly*, October 15, 1989). From other quarters, however, there is the conviction that these fears are exaggerated. Myron B. Kuropas reports in *The Ukrainian Weekly* (July 1, 1990) that Ukrainian Jews he interviewed on a recent trip to Ukraine voiced satisfaction at the avowed commitment of Rukh and the

Ukrainian nationalist movement to combat anti-Semitism in all its forms. "I left Kiev very optimistic about Ukrainian-Jewish relations there. The two groups are supporting each other in their common struggle for human and national rights. They will succeed as long as the KGB within Ukraine, and hate-mongers outside of Ukraine, are not allowed to poison the relationship." Cf. a resolution by Rukh "Against Anti-Semitism," published in *The Ukrainian Weekly* (October 29, 1989).

6. The Law on Freedom of Conscience and Religion was published in *Pravda* on October 9, 1990, and translated into English in a "Special Supplement on Soviet Legislation" kindly supplied by Jane Ellis. It is, to be sure, a matter of dispute just how important this new law is. For example, Albert J. Boiter, an expert on Soviet legislation, believes that the present law is both too late and, given developments in the Soviet Union, likely to be ignored (telephone communication, July 1990). See Boiter's illuminating discussions of earlier drafts of the law on freedom of conscience, "Law and Religion in the Soviet Union," *American Journal of Comparative Law* 35, 1 (1987): 97ff; "Drafting a Freedom of Conscience Law," *Columbia Journal of Transnational Law* 28, 1 (1990): 157ff.

7. Cf. Kolesnyk, "Restructuring the State-Church Relationship," pp. 9-11, and John Anderson, "Further Drafts of New Law on Freedom of Conscience," in *Candle in the Wind: Religion in the Soviet Union,* edited by Eugene B. Shirley, Jr., and Michael Rowe (Washington, D.C.: Ethics and Public Policy Center, 1989), pp. 297-300, for relevant comments on earlier drafts of the law.

8. See John Anderson, "Legislative and Administrative Control of Religious Bodies," in *Candle in the Wind,* p. 69.

2. "Religion and Nationalism"

1. For a succinct articulation of this view of religion by Karl Marx, see "Contribution to the Critique of Hegel's *Philosophy of Right : Introduction,*" in *The Marx-Engels Reader,* edited by Robert C. Tucker, 2nd edition (New York: W. W. Norton & Co., 1978), pp. 53-54.

2. "But whatever form they may have taken, one fact is common to all past ages, viz., the exploitation of one part of society by the other. No wonder, then, that the social consciousness of past ages, despite all the multiplicity and variety it displays, moves within certain common forms, or general ideas, which cannot completely vanish except with the total disappearance of class antagonisms" ("Manifesto of the Communist Party," in *The Marx-Engels Reader,* p. 489).

3. "Critique of the Gotha Program," in *The Marx-Engels Reader*, p. 540. Cf. "Manifesto of the Communist Party," p. 489.

4. V. I. Lenin, *State and Revolution* (New York: International Publishers, 1943), pp. 63–64.

5. Lenin, "The Classes and Parties: Their Attitudes towards Religion," in V. I. Lenin, *Religion* (New York: International Publishers, 1933), p. 25, cited in Bociurkiw, "The Ukrainian Autocephalous Orthodox Church," in *Ukrainian Churches Under Soviet Rule: Two Case Studies* (Cambridge: Ukrainian Studies Fund, Harvard University, 1984), pp. 338–339.

6. "Manifesto of the Communist Party," in *The Marx-Engels Reader*, pp. 488–489.

7. Lenin, *State and Revolution*, p. 29.

8. See our specifications of these terms in the section "About the Series."

9. Bociurkiw, transcript, vol. 1, p. 9: Among several models of Soviet religion policy, the first one was "the model of the new Soviet man, or new Soviet people, a kind of melting pot in ethnic ways.... [A]theist...indoctrination...would eliminate both nationality and religion as obstacles to communism.... [Y]ou cannot enter into communist society with the baggage of nationalism and religion. That model, hopefully, has been laid to rest."

10. The Russian Orthodox church enjoyed a brief period of freedom after the March Revolution in 1917, but that ended abruptly and harshly, as the Bolshevik government placed increasing restrictions on the church, and by the early twenties had begun its policy of persecution. See Jane Ellis, *The Russian Orthodox Church: A Contemporary History* (London: Routledge, 1988), p. 3.

11. Andrew Sorokowski, "Church and State, 1917–64," in *Candle in the Wind*, pp. 27–28. See Michael Rowe, "Religious Persecution and Discrimination," in *Candle in the Wind*, pp. 139–172. See especially the interesting discussion (pp. 167–172) of the various ways of interpreting the policy of discrimination and persecution typically pursued by Soviet governments.

12. "At the request of Stalin's ophthalmologist, one Orthodox church had been left open in Odessa, a city of some 500,000 at the time. Every Sunday a different priest would come forward from the congregation of the church to say Mass, only to be arrested by the police. When there were no more priests, deacons began to appear; when there were no more deacons, psalmists. This went on for some months, until finally the believers were left to worship by themselves" (Sorokowski, "Church and State, 1917–64," in *Candle in the Wind*, p. 40).

13. Bociurkiw, "The Ukrainian Autocephalous Orthodox Church," p. 332.

14. "The events of 1930 dramatized the reversal of Soviet nationality policy, from maintaining a balance between the Russian and Ukrainian nationalisms to a growing reliance on Russian nationalism as an integrating, centralizing force in an increasingly totalitarian regime. The struggle for the ecclesiastical liberation of the Ukraine, the autocephalist 'Away from Moscow,' could no longer be reconciled with the official formula of the 'leading role' of the Russian people, which was now projected from the political sphere onto all the other facets of Russo-Ukrainian relations, including the ecclesiastical-religious sphere" (Bociurkiw, "The Ukrainian Autocephalous Orthodox Church," p. 338).

15. Bociurkiw, "Institutional Religion and Nationality in the Soviet Union," in *Soviet Nationalities in Strategic Perspective*, edited by S. Enders Wimbush (London: Croom Helm, 1985), p. 186.

3. "Beliefs in Conflict"

1. Jane Ellis describes the position of the Russian Orthodox hierarchy as "adopting an attitude of total subservience to the Soviet state, dating... from 1927.... That position has not altered very significantly from 1927 to the present, as far as the church's leadership is concerned" (*Russian Orthodox Church*, p. 261).

2. "The leaders of the Russian Orthodox Church evidently believe that, rather than making futile appeals for greater freedom, it is their duty to do all they can to keep the church alive as an institution, a visible presence, however limited, in Soviet society. They feel that they have a duty to minister to the people, who would have nowhere else to go if even the limited number of presently functioning churches were closed. This is the line the Moscow patriarchate has taken since Metropolitan Sergei's Declaration of 1927, which immediately provoked in the church a deep and bitter schism that persists to this day. In recent times, the late Metropolitan Nikodim, an avowed supporter of Sergei's line, has been the most vigorous proponent of this view. As noted already, this policy necessarily involves repeated falsehood. Dimitri Pospielovsky, a Russian Orthodox historian living in Canada, has recounted a conversation with Nikodim on this question: 'To my remark that it is a bad temptation for a Christian to witness a bishop not telling the truth, he retorted: "It is you people in the West that react this way. We're used to this sort of thing in the Soviet

Union, and we don't react." "But it is terrible," I said, "that lies are accepted in such a way." "I didn't say this was good or bad. I'm just stating a fact," said the Metropolitan with a sad smile. And then he went on to describe his own strategy as that of a man who in dense traffic prefers to select small side roads, and thus a longer distance, while still going toward his aim, rather than get stuck in a traffic jam, or end up in an accident on the main road. He hoped that in this way he would achieve more for the Church in the long run'" (from Ellis, *Russian Orthodox Church*, pp. 274–275).

3. "By the mid-1960s, only 17 or 18 of the 90 Russian Orthodox monastic institutions that had survived since 1917 remained open. In 1960–61 some 10,000 Russian Orthodox churches were closed, and another 5,000 were shut during the next few years. The number of monks and nuns was likewise dramatically reduced, from around 10,000 to some 5,000. By 1965, the 20,000 to 25,000 churches open in 1958 had been reduced to fewer than 8,000. Between the mid-1950s and 1962, the number of diocesan bishops fell from 74 to 63, parish clergy from around 20,000 to about 14,000. The eight seminaries operating in the 1950s were reduced to five by 1962; later, there would be only three" (Sorokowski, "Church and State, 1917–64," in *Candle in the Wind*, p. 58).

4. Sorokowski, "Church and State, 1917–64," in *Candle in the Wind*, p. 49. Metropolitan Sergei Stragorodsky sent a pastoral letter in June 1941 that contained these words: "Our Orthodox church has always shared the fate of the people. It has always borne their trials and cherished their successes. It will not desert the people now. . . . The Church of Christ blesses all the Orthodox defending the sacred frontiers of our motherland. The Lord will grand us victory" (Sorokowski, p. 48).

5. Cited in Bociurkiw, "Institutional Religion and Nationality in the Soviet Union," p. 183.

6. Ellis, "The Russian Orthodox Church's Attitude to the Situation in Ukraine," paper presented to the working group conference, p. 9.

7. In the discussion, Martha Bohachevsky-Chomiak made the following comments: "Let me just be polemical and suggest that the reason for intolerance in the territory, in Ukraine, but especially in Russia, is that the state-not only subjected the churches to its control, but did two other things. It provided special privileges for the Russian Orthodox church, enabling it to buy its freedom at the cost of the freedom of others, and this state-constructed superiority of the Russian Orthodox church has

prevented [it] from really being a truly free Christian church. The other thing the state did was to really institutionalize intolerance, not only institutionalize intolerance, but promote [it]. . .''(transcript, vol. 1, p. 18).

8. See Bociurkiw, ''Politics of Religion in Ukraine,'' p. 26.

9. Hajda, transcript, vol. 1, p. 4: ''One cannot really speak of any divergence of interests between this church and the patriarchate of Moscow. . . . The first steps that have been taken are certainly small and almost laughable if one thinks of introducing Ukrainian as a subject to be studied in seminaries on the territory of Ukraine as a great concession; certainly that does not appear very much.'' Cf. Estocin, ''Summary of Remarks,'' p. 2. In a personal communication (October 17, 1990), Father Webster suggests that the change may be less superficial than Hajda and Estocin think.

10. Hajda, transcript, vol. 1, p. 4: ''But in the future, as [the Ukrainian Orthodox] church has to compete for the loyalties of a more and more nationally conscious Ukrainian population, it may be forced into positions that may pit it. . . [against] the patriarchate of Moscow. . . .''

11. Cited in Father Alexander Webster, *The Price of Prophecy: The Eastern Orthodox Churches on Peace, Freedom, and Security* (Washington D.C.: Ethics and Public Policy Center, forthcoming), p. 103. (I very much appreciate Father Webster's letting me see this chapter from his book.)

12. *Moscow News*, no. 31, 1989, cited in Ellis, ''The Russian Orthodox Church's Attitude,'' p. 4.

13. Ellis, ''The Russian Orthodox Church's Attitude,'' p. 3.

14. ''The bishop of Rome is not [at present] regarded by the Orthodox as a brother bishop or a patriarch in good standing, nor has he [been] since the eleventh century'' (Father Alexander Webster, transcript, vol. 2, p. 14).

15. See Webster, *The Price of Prophecy,* p. 106. Metropolitan Filaret states: ''In March 1946 at the Church's Synod of Lvov [Russian spelling of Lviv], bishops, priests, and lay representatives announced the annulment of the Uniate Church imposed on believers in 1596 a the Synod of Brest. The decision of the Lvov Synod was supported by the overwhelming majority of Greek Catholics, and nearly all the parishes in that region reunited with the Russian Orthodox Church, founded nearly a millennium before by eastern Slavs of Kievan Rus'' (cited in Ellis, ''The Russian Orthodox Church's Attitude,'' p. 3); cf. John Meyendorff, *The Orthodox Church,* 3rd revised ed. (Crestwood, N.Y.: St. Vladimir's Seminary Press, 1981): ''These events, the conditions under which the union with Rome had been imposed, excesses of all kinds, kept alive for centuries a fierce hatred

among the Orthodox faithful toward the authority of Rome, which, in these parts, became identified with that of the Polish kings'' (p. 112). It is hardly necessary to stress that these views are not warmly received by the Ukrainian Catholics. In the conference discussion, Father Webster stated it was important to understand the full scope of official Russian Orthodox attitudes toward the Union of Brest, which were not, he felt, sufficiently stressed in Ellis's paper. This section attempts to give the highlights of those attitudes without, of course, passing judgment on the merits of the arguments (transcript, vol. 2, pp. 14, 15, 16, and 18).

16. Cited by Webster, *The Price of Prophecy,* p. 106.

17. Bishop Ioan of Zhytomyr and Ovruch, ''The Truth about the Union,'' cited in Markus, ''Religion and Nationalism in Ukraine,'' in *Religion and Nationalism in Soviet and East European Politics,* edited by Pedro Ramet (Durham: Duke University Press, 1989), pp. 160–161.

18. Mentioned in Ellis, ''The Russian Orthodox Church's Attitude,'' pp. 4–5.

19. Iaroslav Halan, ''What is Union?'' cited in Bociurkiw, ''The Uniate Church in the Soviet Ukrain: A Case Study in Soviet Church Policy,'' in Bociurkiw, *Ukrainian Churches under Soviet Rule: Two Case Studies* (Cambridge: Ukrainian Studies Fund, 1988), p. 99.

20. ''I am not convinced that the villagers of Western Ukraine are principally motivated by a burning desire to say the *filioque*'' (Ellis, ''The Russian Orthodox Church's Attitude,'' p. 13). On the other hand, Father Webster criticized Ms. Ellis's paper for not paying enough attention to the importance of the *filioque* dispute in the tension that exists. ''The *filioque* is the premier issue of division between all the Orthodox and any other theological community, and it really cannot be downplayed the way it is in the paper. . . . In the Orthodox case, it's absolutely unthinkable [to recite the *filioque*]'' (transcript, vol. 2, p. 14).

21. Webster, *The Price of Prophecy,* p. 106.

22. ''The major event that helped to weaken the opposition to legalization of the Ukrainian Catholic Church was an unprecedented public demonstration in Lviv on September 17, 1989, in which, by Soviet accounts, 'more than 100,000 adherents of the illegal Ukrainian Catholic Church' took part; similar large-scale Uniate demonstrations were held in other West Ukrainian cities.'' Moreover, Ukrainian party leadership was increasingly uncertain about the future status of the Catholic Church. ''Of special importance in exploding the long maintained official myth about an allegedly 'voluntary reunion' of the Greek Catholics with the Russian

Orthodox Church which culminated in the so-called Lviv Sobor of March 1946, were the revelations in the mass circulation *Ognoek* in late September 1989 and in the early October issue of *Argumenty i facty*. These revelations shattered the pretense of canonicity of the Russian Orthodox Church in Galicia and Transcarpathia and were widely perceived as the sure sign of policy change in Moscow'' (Bociurkiw, ''The Problem of Legalization of the Ukrainian Catholic Church in the USSR,'' unpublished paper, pp. 25–26).

23. Markus, ''Religion and Nationalism in Ukraine,'' p. 160.

24. Jaroslav Isayevych, written response to Father Estocin's paper, p. 6: ''I was present at the Millennium scholarly conference organized by the Patriarchate and my paper was the only one devoted to Ukrainian church history. There was no paper in the program devoted to the Belorussian Orthodox.''

25. Webster, transcript, vol. 2, pp. 21–22. Ukrainian Autocephaly is believed to represent the schismatic practice of *philetism*, or an undue emphasis on ''tribal, national differences'' within the church. In 1872, the Council of Constantinople declared, ''Those who accept philetism and dare to found on that basis tribal gatherings we proclaim, in accordance with the Holy Canons, to be alien to the Holy, Catholic and Apostolic Church and being the same as schismatics'' (cited in Ivan Wlasowsky, *Outline History of the Ukrainian Orthodox Church* [New York: Press of the Ukrainian Orthodox Church of USA, 1974], vol. 2, pp. 21–22). In the discussion, Father Webster stressed that so far as the Autocephalous church is concerned, the Russian Orthodox had a legitimate worry about ''the danger of excessive nationalism, expressed as philetism. . . . That the Ukrainian religious communities seem to be drawn into this temptation deserves mention, at least as an unwarranted and disproportionate response to the experience or perception of religious intolerance in Ukraine. . .'' (transcript, vol. 2, p. 15).

It should be noted, however, that members of the Autocephalous church dispute Webster's claim that joint celebration of the liturgy is not allowed, citing several examples to the contrary (private correspondence to the author).

26. Markus, ''Religion and Nationalism in Ukraine,'' p. 140.

27. Radio Liberty research cited in ''Ukraine's Clash of Faiths, '' *Christian Science Monitor,* September 5, 1990, p. 13.

28. Estocin, ''Summary of Remarks,'' p. 1.

29. Bociurkiw, "Politics of Religion in Ukraine," p. 16; cf. Estocin, "Summary of Remarks," p. 1. It should be noted that in the case of Bishop Ioann, the Russian Orthodox church also took the extreme step of stripping him of his monasticism.

30. Webster, transcript, vol. 2, p. 22.

31. Declaration against Intolerance, article 1.1; see Appendix.

32. For specific charges of sedition, see p. 21 above, in which an Orthodox spokesman in 1945 accused the Catholics exploiting the idea of "freedom of religion in order to engage in criminal activities against the Ukrainian people."

33. Declaration against Intolerance, article 2.2; see Appendix.

34. Bociurkiw, "Politics of Religion in Ukraine," p. 10.

35. Ellis, "The Russian Orthodox Church's Attitude," pp. 11-12.

36. This interpretation is drawn from Bociurkiw, "The Uniate Church in the Soviet Ukraine," pp. 104–108, and would, it is assumed, be affirmed by Ukrainian Catholics. Certain further details and elaborations were suggested in a phone conversation with Bociurkiw, July 2, 1990.

37. Bociurkiw, "The Uniate Church in the Soviet Ukraine," pp. 104–108.

38. Bociurkiw, transcript, vol. 2, pp. 5-6, and "The Uniate Church in the Soviet Ukraine," n. 26, p. 96.

39. Bociurkiw, "Politics of Religion in Ukraine," pp. 4-5.

40. Drawn from Webster, *Prophecy or Propaganda?*, p. 108. In the discussion, Father Webster emphasized that insofar as these three demands were uttered unconditionally, they were unreasonable, from a Russian Orthodox point of view. To demand "full recognition" of the Eastern Catholic church would require that the Orthodox "subscribe to Roman Catholic ecclesiology," "something that seems. . . a gratuitous demand at best." To demand that the Russian Orthodox return all property they held as of September 1939 "ignores the past generation of people who have grown in those communities. . . ." And "declaring [the Synod of Lviv] illegal and invalid without any attempt to address the 1596 Union of Brest is also unbalanced and, in short, unreasonable." He complained that there is considerable "anti-Russian vituperation" apparent in public utterances by Ukrainian Catholics that he found unworthy of church officials. And he objected that Jane Ellis's presentation did not attempt to balance the intemperate anti-Catholic remarks by the Russian Orthodox hierarchy with equally intemperate anti-Russian remarks by the Catholics. In response, Jane Ellis defended her attempt to understand Russian

Orthodox grievances. She went on: "If I'm being oversympathetic to the Ukrainian side, I think there are grounds for that, and I think there are grounds for not expecting people to emerge overnight from a catacomb situation. . . able to take an equal part with others who have been left disadvantaged. And I would urge a charitable interpretation of these central nonnegotiable demands in light of that." In short, she suggested that that "anti-Russian vituperation" was understandable against the experience of the Ukrainian Catholic Church, and not likely "to stop overnight." "We may need to wait for a new generation to come along" (transcript, vol. 2, pp. 15–16).

41. Bociurkiw, transcript, vol. 1, p. 24.

42. Cited by Bociurkiw in "The Ukrainian Autocephalous Orthodox Church," p. 320.

43. "On October 23, Archpriest Vasil Lypkivsky (b. 1864), the spiritual leader of the Ukrainian national church movement and one of the organizers of the All-Ukrainian Church Council. . .was ordained Metropolitan of Kiev and All Ukraine through a laying-on of hands by the clerical and lay members of the sobor. Then jointly with the sobor members, Metropolitan Lypkivsky consecrated Archpriest Nestor Sharaivsky as another bishop and, late in October, the two hierarchs ordained four other priests as bishops for several Ukrainian dioceses. This departure from the established Orthodox procedures, as well as a series of canonical reforms adopted by the 1921 sobor, not only alienated some clerical supporters of the movement, but also resulted in a virtual isolation of the [UAOC] from other Orthodox churches which refused to recognize the canonic validity of its episcopate" (Bociurkiw, "The Orthodox Church in Ukraine since 1917," in *Ukraine: A Concise Encyclopedia*, [Toronto: University of Toronto Press, 1971], vol. 2, p. 170).

44. See Frank E. Sysyn, *The Ukrainian Orthodox Question in the USSR*, The Millennium Series (Cambridge: Ukrainian Studies Fund, Harvard University, 1987), p. 12.

45. The fifth principle is the objective of "Christianizing" the social order, or applying to social life Christian ideals of love, justice, forbearance, and so on.

46. This statement by Archbishop M. Pyvovariv, made in 1928, is cited in Bociurkiw, "The Ukrainian Autocephalous Orthodox Church," pp. 324–325. Bociurkiw mentions that there was some division within the synod over how far to go in asserting the compatibility between the church and the government. Still, the declaration announces that "the church is not a political organization and cannot assume any party or state functions...."

47. Ibid., p. 325. See Wlasowsky, *Outline History of the Ukrainian Orthodox Church*, vol. 1, pp. 9–18, for a theological and scriptural defense of the constructive relation between nationality and religion.

48. Bociurkiw, "The Ukrainian Autocephalous Orthodox Church," p. 326. Metropolitan Mstyslav, who was in the audience at the conference, made the following comments: "Ukraine is to this day not independent.... Unfortunately, all decisions that are made pertinent to religious life in Ukraine, pertinent to religious freedom in Ukraine, need not only the approval of Kiev or of the authorities in Kiev, but these petitions that are being submitted by various religious communities in Ukraine still have to be forwarded to Moscow, for the approval of either the Holy Synod of the Russian Orthodox Church or the secular authorities. During the Tsarist regime, the Russian Orthodox Church was an instrument for colonization..." (transcript, vol. 1, p. 23).

49. Bociurkiw, "The Ukrainian Autocephalous Orthodox Church," p. 327.

50. Ibid. Bociurkiw mentions that the attempt to graft a democratic polity onto a more autocratic form of church government resulted in some deep tensions in the church.

51. Cited in Sysyn, "The Ukrainian Orthodox Question," p. 257.

52. "Orthodox Church Synod Proclaims Mstyslav Patriarch of Ukraine," *The Ukrainian Weekly*, June 10, 1990, pp. 1, 11.

53. In an appearance at the conference at the Institute on June 20, 1990, when he made a number of public comments (transcript, vol. 1, p. 23).

54. "Metropolitan Ioann Discusses the Ukrainian Autocephalous Church Today," *The Ukrainian Weekly*, October 14, 1990, pp. 3, 14.

55. Quoted in *The Ukrainian Weekly*, June 10, 1990, p. 1.

56. Transcript, vol. 1, pp. 22–23 (and untranscribed comments on accompanying tape) for Metropolitan Mstyslav's support for freedom of religion. *The Ukrainian Weekly*, October 14, 1990, p. 14 for the sentiments of Metropolitan Ioann. Cf. comments by Metropolitan Ioann reported in *The Ukrainian Weekly*, October 29, 1989, pp. 1, 14: "I would like to define my relations to our brothers and sisters in faith and in blood—the Ukrainian Catholics. I feel they have every right to the recognition of their faith and I express the hope that among the Ukrainian Orthodox and

Ukrainian Churches there will be brotherly relations, contacts of peace and love, as was preached by our Lord, Jesus Christ.''

57. Conversation with Bociurkiw in October 1990 after his return from a trip to Ukraine.

58. Ibid.

4. "Strife of the Churches"

1. In "Politics of Religion in Ukraine," Bociurkiw used the number 1,000 rather than 800. In a phone conversation on January 5, 1991, he corrected the number based on new information.

2. Bociurkiw, "Politics of Religion in Ukraine," pp. 21–22.

3. Cited in Ellis, "The Russian Orthodox Church's Attitude," p. 6.

4. Ibid.

5. "Russian Orthodox Hierarch in Kiev Fears Spiritual Chernobyl in Ukraine," *The Ukrainian Weekly*, April 29, 1990, p. 3.

6. Linda Feldman, "Ukraine's Clash of Faiths," *Christian Science Monitor*, September 5, 1990, pp. 12–13.

7. Ellis, "The Russian Orthodox Church's Attitude," p. 6.

8. William B.Montalbano, "Pope Urges Ukrainian Church to Reconcile with Orthodox," *Washington Post*, June 25, 1990.

9. FBIS-SOV-90-067, April 6, 1990, pp. 100–101.

10. FBIS-SOV-90-043, March 5, 1990, p. 110.

11. Ellis, "The Russian Orthodox Church's Attitude," p. 7.

12. Ellis, transcript, vol. 2, p. 16.

13. Webster, transcript, vol. 2, pp. 14–15.

14. Kolesnyk, transcript, vol. 2, pp. 3–4.

15. Ibid., p. 10. Kolesnyk mentions that recognition of the Ukrainian Catholic hierarchy would depend on the bishops having "official approval from their religious center, in this case Rome...that approves them as hierarchy, and as such it has not been approved to date." On June 25–26, 1990, the Pope in fact confirmed the ordination of the Ukrainian Catholics as valid, thereby providing the basis for their authority. The Soviet government's response at this point is not known.

16. Kolesnyk, transcript, vol. 3, p. 6.

17. Ibid., p. 9. Kolesnyk stated that the leasing policy is not being addressed in the new draft laws and would not likely be changed. However, according to Bociurkiw (in a private conversation), there is some prospect for change in that regard under the influence of the democratic bloc at the level of the Ukrainian Supreme Soviet.

18. "Soviet Archbishop Pushes for Change" (an article discussing a recent visit to the United States by the Reverend Kirill Gundiaev, Russian Orthodox archbishop of Smolensk and director of the church's Department of External Affairs), *Washington Post*, June 2, 1990.

19. Estocin, "Summary of Remarks," p. 1.

20. Bociurkiw, "Politics of Religion in Ukraine," p. 27.

21. Press report of October 28, 1990, translated from a Ukrainian newspaper by Lubomyr Hajda.

22. Postconference conversation with Father Estocin.

23. Interview with Metropolitan Ioann, *The Ukrainian Weekly*, October 14, 1990, p. 3. According to Bociurkiw (phone conversation, January 5, 1991), Metropolitan Ioann overstates the numbers. *Radianska Ukraina* (November 4, 1990) reports that currently about 500 priests provide leadership for about 1,043 Autocephalous parishes, all but ten of which are in Galicia.

24. FBIS-SOV-90-209, October 29, 1990, p. 100. Cf. "Thousands in Kiev Attempt to Block St. Sophia Sobor," *The Ukrainian Weekly*, November 4, 1990, p. 1.

25. Official Kremlin international news broadcast, Federal News Service, October 29, 1990.

26. Hajda, transcript, vol. 1, p. 5. See Bociurkiw, "The Problem of Legalization," p. 33.

27. Interview with Metropolitan Ioann, *The Ukrainian Weekly*, October 14, 1990, pp. 3, 14. These statements are strongly disputed by observers such as Bociurkiw. There is no support for the claim that "six, seven [Catholic] parishes went over to the UAOC." Nor is there evidence for the charge that Catholics have appropriated churches in which they have been allowed to worship (phone conversation with Bociurkiw, January 5, 1991).

28. Translated from a Ukrainian newspaper by Lubomyr Hajda.

29. Reported by Bociurkiw in a phone conversation, July 2, 1990. Cf. *The Ukrainian Weekly*, April 29, 1990: "More Than 400 Apply for Training to Become Ukrainian Catholic Priests."

30. "The Church That Broke Its Silence," *The Financial Times*, September 4, 1990, p. 19.

31. These thoughts about the present political climate were conveyed in a private conversation with Bociurkiw. Hajda briefly discusses the role of the state authorities at the local, republican, and central administrative levels, transcript, vol. 1, p. 5.

5. "Continuing Sources of Conflict"

1. Francis Deng put the question this way in the discussion: "[All this] really raises the question in one's mind as to how we delineate this whole project; where you cut off the emphasis on the religious aspect of intolerance, and even ideology, and where, as in the case. . .of Lebanon and the Sudan, . . . religion [is just] an element in the concept of identity. [I]dentity is not an isolated issue; it becomes an essential feature of the whole political, cultural, economic relations of [the] conflict in a very broad sense" (transcript, vol.1, p. 8). Jaroslav Isayevych agreed: "I suppose that the question of the relationship between ethnicity, nationality and religion is perhaps the crucial question for this panel and for this conference" (p. 10).

2. Isayevych, transcript, vol. 1, pp. 10–11.

3. Ibid. This slight reconstruction of Isayevych's comments seems to represent fairly the point he intends to make.

4. As suggested especially by Bocirukiw in the discussion (transcript, vol. 1, pp. 8–10).

5. See p. 19, above.

6. Bocirukiw, transcript, vol. 1, p. 9.

7. Ibid.

8. "As long as people continue to see the connection between the central administrative structure in Moscow. . .and the Russian Orthodox Church, it will be very difficult to separate the issue of Orthodoxy from lack of political control as such. . ." (Bohachevsky-Chomiak, transcript, vol. 1, p. 19).

9. "I must confess that, despite the richness [of the discussion so far] I find it almost vacuous in terms of what it tells a sociologist. And especially since [we] will be concerned to look at Ukraine in comparison to other countries. First, who is a believer? You talk about numbers of believers—are they church goers? Who [is labeled] as a believer? Is it state-imposed, or is it based on certain perceptions, certain admissions, on the intensity of one's faith, on the intensity of one's beliefs, or is it simply a label that comes and goes? Two, . . . how do these groups perceive themselves? . . . You walk into the streets of Beirut, and you can tell who are the Shi'ites, who are the Maronites, who are the Sunnis, who are the Druze there. You can tell a lot about not only what I call the ecology of fear, but the social-economic indicators, in their marriage, schooling, residence, every single parameter seems to be related to a religious identity. . . . [In our discussion,] I hear very little about this. . . . I don't know how these definitions of recognizing a group, registering a group [work, including the] . . . feelings, sentiments, attitudes about people. . . . [F]or people concerned about future prospects, how do these perceptions affect, how do we move from intolerance to pluralism, and how would this pluralism, this new national identity incline to be defined?'' (Samir Khalaf, transcript, vol. 2, pp. 5–6).

10. Bociurkiw, transcript, vol. 2, p. 6.

11. Isayevych, written response to Father Estocin's paper, p. 8.

12. Bociurkiw, transcript, vol. 1, p. 12. Cf. Bohachevsky-Chomiak: "Under the Soviets, but also under the Tsar, you do have the erosion of historical memory, and the specific doctrines of certain historical facts." There is, however, the same sense of tradition maintained among the Ukrainian Catholics as well as the Orthodox by means of church pageantry. "This is what I witnessed in the Easter holidays in Ukraine a couple of months ago—the specific way in which the pageantry of the church was used as just one other means of expression of the wealth of the spiritual culture" (transcript, vol. 2, p. 9).

13. Bociurkiw, transcript, vol. 2, p. 8.

14. "[A] major [cause of] intolerance and even mutual hatred [is] the one-sided interpretation of the historical past. Many Polish Catholic historians describe the Polish-Lithuanian Commonwealth as an example of religious tolerance and equality of all ethnic communities. On the other side, Ukrainian Orthodox and Greek Catholic authors pay much attention to the discrimination [against] the Eastern Christian population in the Commonwealth. Ukrainian Orthodox, like most of the Orthodox, like to repeat in their scholarly and popular publications that this discrimination was performed not only by Polish Roman Catholics, but also by Ukrainian Uniates. But it should be noted that Ukrainian Catholic authors while writing much about persecution of the Uniates by Russian authorities, do not

stress either the persecution of Uniates by the Ukrainian Cossacks nor the fact that Greek Catholicism was banned in the Ukrainian autonomous state, the Hetmanate. Although the juridical situation of the Uniates in the Hetmanate was much worse than that of the Orthodox in the Polish Kingdom, even Ukrainian Catholic historians deplore more the discrimination of the Ukrainian Orthodox population by foreign Catholic rulers than the persecution of the Ukrainian Uniates at the hands of their Orthodox compatriots.

''On the other side, Ukrainian Catholics are much more biased when they deny any positive contribution of the Orthodox clergy in the modern Ukrainian revival in the . . . early twentieth century. Among Ukrainian Catholic clergy and lay activists there exist biased opinions purporting an overall ignorance of the Orthodox clergy'' (Isayevych, written response to Father Estocin's paper, pp. 7–8).

15. See Metropolitan Filaret's comments above, pp. 19–20.

16. The observers in question are especially Ellis, Bociurkiw, and Bohachevsky-Chomiak. It is not entirely clear whether the argument presented by Webster in ''What the Media Have Missed in Eastern Europe,'' *Washington Post*, July 31, 1990, is opposed to the recommendations of Ellis, Bociurkiw, and Bohachevsky-Chomiak. In general, he accuses the press of indulging in an oversimplified and one-sided interpretation of history that unfairly favors one party over another in the myriad of ethnic and religious conflicts present in Eastern Europe and the Soviet Union. In regard specifically to Ukraine, Webster accuses journalists of honoring only the Ukrainian Catholics, and the Ukrainian nationalist account of who wronged whom, without remembering that the Russians and the Russian Orthodox church have also been victims at times. ''[T]he shameless shilling for Ukrainian nationalism in the press is often accompanied by an unconscionable bashing of all things Russian, including the Russian Orthodox Church.'' On the other hand, Webster makes a remark that appears to imply the need for concessions of the sort recommended by Ellis, Bociurkiw, and Bohachevsky-Chomiak: ''Certainly, none of the foregoing should be construed as a justification for the more recent undemocratic villainy by some of these Orthodox peoples against their neighbors.''

17. Ellis, transcript, vol. 2, p. 13. Cf. Bociurkiw, transcript, vol. 1, p. 24, and Bohachevsky-Chomiak, transcript, vol. 1, pp. 18–21.

18. John Kelsay, postconference communication, p. 2.

19. "It is hard to resolve disagreements about memory, in part because they are so personal" (Ellis, transcript, vol. 2, p. 3). Ellis mentions in the same context that, according to Russian friends of hers, it may be necessary to wait another generation for genuinely revisionist interpretations to be widely embraced.

20. Kolesnyk, transcript, vol. 1, p. 24.

21. Kolesnyk, transcript, vol. 3, p. 1. "[The Russian Orthodox Church is not, strictly speaking, privileged,] but [has] the stronger hand, . . .the advantageous position, from the viewpoint of Soviet law. . ." (transcript, vol. 3, p. 6).

22. Kolesnyk, transcript, vol. 1, p. 24. At transcript, vol. 2, pp. 16–17, he continues: "If it had been, hypothetically, in 1946. . .that all the churches which were then practicing Greek Catholic religion, if all those churches had been handed over to some imported Orthodox leader, and those who had been previously practicing Greek Catholic religion, if they had been made to convene secretly, . . .those newcomers had been given those churches to practice the Orthodox religion there, if it had been that way, there could have been some reason to say that that Orthodox church has to be ousted from those places. But what in fact has taken place is that, simply, after that, those Greek Catholic churches, they were just formed into Orthodox churches, and those very parishes, those very communities, they practiced Orthodox religion. Now, [t]he majority of those who are now voicing their positions to the Orthodox religion, . . . most of them were baptized [forty-four years ago] in those very churches, most of them were married by the priests of those Orthodox, churches. *So there is no moral right to say that now the Orthodox, or the Russian Orthodox, or the Ukrainian Orthodox, should be ousted from those places . . .*" (emphasis added).

23. Donna Sullivan, transcript, vol. 2, p. 10.

24. Gerald Powers, transcript, vol. 2, p. 19.

25. See especially pp. 19–20, above, for Metropolitan Filaret's claims that the Uniate church is an "artificial" church and that it was part of an "unnatural union" that was "a source of national, social and religious oppression."

26. The account in this section draws heavily on Bociurkiw, "The Politics of Religion in Ukraine," pp. 22–25.

27. Ibid., pp. 23–24. Commenting on this meeting, Jane Ellis points out that the Russian Orthodox church appointed only one delegate, although they might have had two. That fact, together with the questionable character of the man they sent, "'suggests a lack of enthusiasm on the part of the ROC for the mission to Ukraine. . . . Metropolitan [Sterniuk] appears to have blamed both the ROC and the Vatican delegation for falling in too readily with what the ROC had told them. According to Father Ivan Dacko, secretary to the head of the UGCC, Cardinal Lubachivsky, who resides in Rome, a series of actions by the Orthodox side offended the UGCC leader. For example, the Orthodox were not willing to discuss points of principle such as the status of the 1946 Synod of Lviv, but only the future designation of individual churches. As the commission began to make its way around Western Ukraine, the Orthodox were able to telephone ahead to find where crowds were gathering, and were thus able to avoid locations where there were large numbers of Catholics waiting'' (''The Russian Orthodox Church's Attitude,'' pp. 7–8).

28. ''Church Officials Discuss Conflict in Ukraine,'' FBIS-SOV-90-180, September 17, 1990, p. 102.

29. ''Moscow Patriarchate Breaks Off Meeting with Ukrainian Catholics, Vatican Representatives. Orthodox Demand Transfiguration Church, Chapel of Cathedral of St. George and Cathedral in Ivano-Frank-vsk,'' Press Office of the Ukrainian Catholic Church, Rome, September 18, 1990.

30. ''Metropolitan Ioann Discusses the Ukrainian Autocephalous Orthodox Church Today,'' *The Ukrainian Weekly*, October 14, 1990, p. 14.

31. Ibid. Metropolitan Ioann continues, ''I think that the hierarchs of both the Ukrainian Autocephalous Orthodox Church and the Ukrainian Greek Catholic Church can find a common language between them. Until this time, we have not had any contact in terms of cooperation. I, for example, looked for such contacts, but did not find it from Metropolitan Sterniuk. I think, I even believe, that upon my return from America, we will get together and discuss such questions.''

32. ''Ukrainian Catholics and Ukrainian Orthodox on many occasions have manifested and shown to the world that they are worthy Christians, and I believe that such cooperation would be possible, even today, if the third party [the Soviet government] did not have its hands in this game. . . . I fully believe that the confessional conflict is being fueled either from above or from down below by the lower elements of society. . .'' (Mstyslav, transcript, vol. 1, p. 23).

6. ''Conclusion''

1. Orest Vlohk, member of Parliament and a regional leader of Rukh, transcript, vol. 1, pp. 24–25: ''In our situation, it is perfectly all right for all religions to exist and coexist, and it should be the understanding that all of them make up the totality of Ukrainian culture."

2. Article 2 prohibits a "preference based on religion or belief and having as its. . .effect. . .impairment of the. . .exercise of human rights. . .on an equal basis."

3. See pp. 60–61, above.

4. Ibid.

5. See p. 36, above.

6. Bociurkiw, transcript, vol. 1, p. 10. Bohachevsky-Chomiak observed: "[M]aybe the traditional formulation of church-state separation worked in the nineteenth century, but may in the twentieth century, what we need to stress is that [none] of the agencies, [none] of the items that define our self-consciousness, can claim full and complete control, and full and complete truth. . . . Maybe that would be a more useful paradigm than church-state separation. . . . [In the United States] none of the ideologies, none of the systems of belief. . .can or should. . .make a claim to absolute truth. . ." (transcript, vol. 2, p. 23). Gerald Powers remarked: "What I think is needed is not that you would somehow sanitize religion or put it off to the sidelines, but that society somehow agrees that belief is a good thing. . .but that religion does not become equated with any particular economic or political system" (transcript, vol. 2, p. 26).

7. Several members of the working group emphasized these problems. For example, Elliot Sperling commented: "A larger part of this question, of the interrelationship of religion and politics, is a very, very modern question. . . . In modern times, we seem to be getting away from this [intertwining], and it's a luxury for us to speak about trying to depoliticize religion, or to try and take religion out of the political system, because to a certain extent we [Americans] live in a society in which the force of organized religion is considerably diminished. . . . It's a very complex issue, and it really comes down to different societies at different levels of development" (transcript, vol. 2, p. 23).

8. Mark Juergensmeyer wondered whether, in considering whether pluralist models are relevant to cases like Ukraine, we must face "some unfinished business of the Enlightenment, because behind the American pluralist experiment is a social one, with the ideological notion that such a congeries of ethnic communities could be held together by a new legitimation of the state, based not on religion, but on reason and the will of the people. . . . [I]n a pessimistic reading of the present situation, there's

a kind of collapse of belief in the temple of reason, of the state, . . . in many parts of the world, whether it's a Marxist framework or an American parliamentary one. . ." (transcript, vol. 2, pp. 23–24).

9. Andrew Sorokowski, "Beyond the Fortress Church: The Role of the Church, Religion in Ukraine and Ukrainian Diaspora," in *The Ukrainian Weekly*, February 11, 1990. Having mentioned "a pessimistic reading" of the future of Western models of pluralism (see note 8, above), Juergensmeyer then went on to suggest a more "positive reading" of the possibilities in Ukraine: "The unfinished business. . . now being worked through, that whatever form of Ukrainian church, whether it's Ukrainian Catholic or Autocephalous or the Orthodox Church connected with Moscow, . . . will in some way be joined with a notion of a tolerant nationalism that has within it. . . several different levels of loyalty, where one can begin to sort out cultural loyalties from specific [institutional] loyalties. . ." (transcript, vol. 2, pp. 23–24).

"Afterword"

1. Interview with Ivan Hrechko, chairman of the Commission on Religious Freedom of Rukh, Lviv chapter, on December 13, 1990, at the United States Institute of Peace. Translation was kindly supplied by Irene Jarosevich. The author is grateful to Mr. Hrechko for taking time to provide material that very much updates the description of events contained in this report.

2. Mr. Hrechko's opinion is that as soon as "the local, Moscow-controlled Communist Party began to lose ground in the local districts of western Ukraine, the Russian Orthodox Church also began to lose ground. These two groups went hand in hand together."

3. According to Mr. Hrechko, the claim for total restitution "was always a position of principle; it was theoretical. Realistically and practically they always understood that they would not get everything they demanded. At the time it was necessary to state that a wrong had happened, that it had been theft, and that the property should be returned. . . . But [now] the Catholic Church is simply going after specific, individual properties. . . . The church is asking for their return and they are being returned. [The church also recognizes that the newly elected democratic governments at the local level] really had nothing to do with the problem, and therefore are not responsible for compensation."

4. Mr. Hrechko's own words.

5. According to Mr. Hrechko, the charges by the Catholics of outside Soviet influence on the activities of the Autocephalous Orthodox have some basis in fact. He is puzzled why the Autocephalous church concentrates all its efforts in the west and neglects eastern Ukraine, where its historic support resides unless it is being prompted to do so for ulterior reasons. Moreover, ''the very slurs used by the Autocephalous against the Catholics [about disloyalty to Ukraine] are the same slurs verbatim that were used by the Russian Orthodox hierarchy [against the Catholics]. . . . [Finally, some of the most outspoken Autocephalous hierarchs] are the very same people who were so tightly involved for a long time with the Russian Orthodox hierarchy.''

6. Mr. Hrechcko's own words.

7. Mr. Hrechko projects that the new constitution will be completed and adopted after the next general elections in February 1992. He says that those in charge of producing the draft pay little attention to President Gorbachev's call for completion of new republican constitutions by the end of 1990 to address the question of a new all-union treaty among the republics.

The Ukraine Conference

This report is based on a conference, "Ukraine: The Threat of Intolerance and the Promise of Pluralism," that took place at the United States Institute of Peace on June 20 and 21, 1990.

The conference was organized around four major paper presenters. Bohdan R. Bociurkiw, professor of political science at Carleton University in Ottawa, Canada, delivered a paper entitled "The Politics of Religion in Ukraine under Gorbachev: The Case of the Ukrainian Greek Catholic Church." Professor Bociurkiw is a specialist in Soviet politics with a long-standing research interest that includes Soviet religious policy, especially in Ukraine, as well as church-state relations in Eastern Europe. He has published numerous monographs and articles on these subjects. He was born in Ukraine and comes from a Ukrainian Catholic background.

Jane Ellis, senior researcher at Keston College, England, presented a paper entitled "The Russian Orthodox Church's Attitude to the Situation in Ukraine." Ms. Ellis is author of a definitive book on the Russian Orthodox church and is a leading expert on that subject.

Mikola Panasovych Kolesnyk, chairman of the Council of Religious Affairs of the Council of Ministers of the Ukrainian SSR, presented a paper entitled "Restructuring the State-to-Church Relationship, and Paths toward the Normalization of the Religious Situation in Ukraine." Mr. Kolesnyk represented the perspective of the Soviet government.

Father Frank Estocin, dean of St. Vladimir Ukrainian Catholic Cathedral in Philadelphia and rector of St. Sophia Ukrainian Orthodox Seminary in South Bound Brook, New Jersey, submitted a paper, "Summary of Remarks Concerning the Ukrainian Autocephalous Church," but was unable to attend the conference because of a death in the family.

Four respondents participated. Martha Bohachevsky-Chomiak is program officer for scholarly translations at the National Endowment for the

Humanities and a visiting professor at several universities. She is the author of a study of women in Ukrainian community life, and is herself of Ukrainian extraction. Lubomyr Hajda, fellow at the Russian Research Center at Harvard and academic coordinator of the Soviet Union Regional Studies Program, is author of several articles and coeditor of a book on the nationalities problem in the Soviet Union. He is also of Ukrainian extraction. Jaroslav Isayevych, director of the Institute of Social Sciences of the Academy of Sciences of the Ukrainian SSR and a former visiting scholar at the Harvard Ukrainian Research Institute, is author of numerous publications on medieval Ukrainian culture and lives in Ukraine. Father Alexander Webster is a priest in the Romanian Orthodox church, a fellow at the Ethics and Public Policy Center in Washington, D.C., and author of several publications on ethics and policy in the Orthodox tradition.

Because the conference took place in June 1990, the description of events contained in this report was largely determined by the state of affairs in Ukraine at that time, although some attempt has been made to include references to subsequent events. These references are based on reports of recent visits to Ukraine by Bohdan Bociurkiw as well as material supplied by Lubomyr Hajda; they are also drawn from sources such as *The Ukrainian Weekly* and the Foreign Broadcast Information Service for the Soviet Union. Accordingly, some of the conclusions and central observations that emerged from the conference have been updated in the report. (The actual transcript of the conference as well as the papers presented there have been deposited with the library of the United States Institute of Peace.)

Still, the situation in Ukraine was so fluid, and certain features emphasized in the report so subject to change, that it was thought advisable to include an afterword that would further update the description of events and highlight the changes that appear to be taking place. Material for the afterword was supplied by the chairman of the Commission on Religious Freedom of Rukh (the Ukrainian People's Movement for Perestroika) in an illuminating interview conducted at the Institute in mid-December 1990.

The author bears the full and final responsibility for the views expressed in this report. The views do not represent the position of the United States Institute of Peace or, necessarily, that of any of the people associated with the conference, some of whom may not be entirely satisfied with the final contents of this report.

The author acknowledges the generous assistance of all those who participated in the conference. Without the help of the members of the Working Group on Religion, Ideology, and Peace and the speakers and respondents, the preparation of this report would have been impossible. Their various suggestions for revising early drafts were very helpful.

Special thanks must go to Bohdan Bociurkiw, who provided invaluable assistance in planning the conference, in providing background material, and, finally, in carefully reviewing and revising the report. Lubomyr Hajda went well beyond the call of duty. His suggestions for restructuring parts of the report and for adding crucial historical materials have immeasurably strengthened the final product. The author is also particularly indebted to Jane Ellis, Father Webster, and Martha Bohachevsky-Chomiak for their useful suggestions. Finally, Barry Seltser, former research assistant for the working group, and Darrin McMahon, the present assistant, rendered outstanding service in producing this report. Mr. McMahon's editorial assistance was indispensable.

Appendix: UN Declaration Against Intolerance

Resolution Adopted by the General Assembly [on the Report of the Third Committee (A/36/684)] 36/55. *Declaration on the Elimination of All Forms of Intolerance and of Discrimination Based on Religion or Belief.*

Considering that one of the basic principles of the Charter of the United Nations is that of the dignity and equality inherent in all human beings, and that all Member States have pledged themselves to take joint and separate action in co-operation with the Organization to promote and encourage universal respect for the observance of human rights and fundamental freedoms for all, without distinction as to race, sex, language or religion,

Considering that the Universal Declaration on Human Rights [General Assembly Resolution 217A (III)] and the International Covenants on Human Rights [General Assembly Resolution 2200A (XXI)] proclaim the principles of non-discrimination and equality before the law and the right to freedom of thought, conscience, religion and belief,

Considering that the disregard and infringement of human rights and fundamental freedoms, in particular of the right to freedom of thought, conscience, religion or whatever belief, have brought, directly or indirectly, wars and great suffering to mankind, especially where they serve as a means of foreign interference in the internal affairs of other States and amount to kindling hatred between peoples and nations,

Considering that religion or belief, for anyone who professes either, is one of the fundamental elements in his conception of life and that freedom of religion or belief should be fully respected and guaranteed,

Considering that it is essential to promote understanding, tolerance and respect in matters relating to freedom of religion and belief to ensure that the use of religion or belief for ends inconsistent with the Charter, other relevant instruments of the United Nations and the purposes and principles of the present Declaration is inadmissable,

Convinced that freedom of religion and belief should also contribute to the attainment of the goals of world peace, social justice and friendship among peoples and to the elimination of ideologies or practices of colonialism and racial discrimination,

Noting with satisfaction the adoption of several, and the coming force of some, conventions, under the aegis of the United Nations and of the specialized agencies, for the elimination of various forms of discrimination,

Concerned by manifestations of intolerance and by the existence of discrimination in matters of religion or belief still in evidence in some areas of the world,

Resolved to adopt all necessary measures for the speedy elimination of such intolerance in all its forms and manifestations and to prevent and combat discrimination on the grounds of religion of belief,

Proclaims this Declaration on the Elimination of All Forms of Intolerance and of Discrimination Based on Religion or Belief:

Article 1

1. Everyone shall have the right to freedom of thought, conscience and religion. This right shall include freedom to have a religion or whatever belief of his choice, and freedom, either individually or in community with others, and in public or private, to manifest his religion or belief in worship, observance, practice and teaching.

2. No one shall be subject to coercion which would impair his freedom to have a religion or belief of his choice.

3. Freedom to manifest one's religion or beliefs may be subject only to such limitations as are prescribed by law and are necessary to protect public safety, order, health or morals or the fundamental rights and freedoms of others.

Article 2

1. No one shall be subject to discrimination by any State, institution, group of persons or person on the grounds of religion or other beliefs.

2. For the purposes of the present Declaration, the expression "intolerance and discrimination based on religion or belief" means any distinction, exclusion, restriction or preference based on religion or belief and having as its purpose or as its effect nullification or impairment of the recognition, enjoyment or exercise of human rights and fundamental freedoms on an equal basis.

Article 3

Discrimination between human beings on the grounds of religion or belief constitutes an affront to human dignity and a disavowal of the principles of the Charter of the United Nations, and shall be condemned as a violation of the human rights and fundamental freedoms proclaimed in the Universal Declaration on Human Rights and enunciated in detail in the International Covenants on Human Rights, and as an obstacle to friendly and peaceful relations between nations.

Article 4

1. All States shall take effective measures to prevent and eliminate discrimination on the grounds of religion or belief in the recognition, exercise and enjoyment of human rights and fundamental freedoms in all fields of civil, economic, political, social and cultural life.

2. All States shall make all efforts to enact or rescind legislation where necessary to prohibit any such discrimination, and take all appropriate measures to combat intolerance on the grounds of religion or other beliefs in this matter.

Article 5

1. The parents or, as the case may be, the legal guardians of the child have the right to organize the life within the family in accordance with their religion or belief and bearing in mind the moral education in which they believe the child should be brought up.

2. Every child shall enjoy the right to have access to education in the matter of religion or belief in accordance with the wishes of his parents or legal guardians, the best interests of the child being the guiding principle.

3. The child shall be protected from any form of discrimination on the grounds of religion or belief. He shall be brought up in a spirit of

understanding, tolerance, friendship among peoples, peace and universal brotherhood, respect for freedom of religion or belief of others, and in full consciousness that his energy and talents should be devoted to the service of his fellow men.

4. In the case of a child who is not under the care either of his parents or of legal guardians, due account shall be taken of their expressed wishes or of any other proof of their wishes in the matter of religion or belief, the best interests of the child being the guiding principle.

5. Practices of a religion or beliefs in which a child is brought up must not be injurious to his physical or mental health or to his full development, taking into account article 1, paragraph 3, of the present Declaration.

Article 6

In accordance with article 1 of the present Declaration, and subject to the provisions of article 1, paragraph 3, the right to freedom of thought, conscience, religion or belief shall include, inter alia, the following freedoms:

(a) To worship or assemble in connexion with a religion or belief, and to establish and maintain places for these purposes;

(b) To establish and maintain appropriate charitable or humanitarian institutions;

(c) To make, acquire and use to an adequate extent the necessary articles and materials related to the rites or customs of a religion or belief;

(d) To write, issue and disseminate relevant publications in these areas;

(e) To teach a religion or belief in places suitable for these purposes;

(f) To solicit and receive voluntary financial and other contributions from individuals and institutions;

(g) To train, appoint, elect or designate by succession appropriate leaders called for by the requirements and standards of any religion or belief;

(h) To observe days of rest and to celebrate holidays and ceremonies in accordance with the precepts of one's religion or belief;

(i) To establish and maintain communications with individuals and communities in matters of religion and belief at the national and international levels.

Article 7

The rights and freedoms set forth in the present Declaration shall be accorded in national legislations in such a manner that everyone shall be able to avail himself of such rights and freedoms in practice.

Article 8

Nothing in the present Declaration shall be construed as restricting or derogating from any right defined in the Universal Declaration on Human Rights and the International Covenants on Human Rights.

73rd plenary meeting
25 November 1981

Members of the Working Group on Religion, Ideology, and Peace

Kevin Avruch is a professor of sociology at George Mason University, Fairfax,Virginia. He specializes in Israeli society and politics.

Bohdan R. Bociurkiw is a professor in the Department of Political Science at Carleton College, Ottawa, Canada. Bociurkiw is an expert in the politics of religion in Ukraine.

Francis Deng is a senior fellow at the Brookings Institution, Washington, D.C. A former distinguished fellow at the United States Institute of Peace, Deng focuses on religious and ethnic conflict in Sudan.

Patti Gossman is a research associate at Asia Watch, Washington, D.C. In addition to a general knowledge of human rights issues, Gossman also has expertise in the politics of southern Asia.

Lubomyr Hajda is a professor at the Russian Research Center, Harvard University, Cambridge, Massachusetts. Hajda's areas of specialization include the role of religion in the society and politics of Ukraine.

Hurst Hannum is a professor of international law at the Fletcher School of Law and Diplomacy, Medford, Massachusetts. A former peace fellow at the United States Institute of Peace, Hannum is an expert in human rights law and minority rights, subjects on which he has written extensively.

James Turner Johnson is university director of international programs at Rutgers University, New Brunswick, New Jersey. Johnson has strong expertise in Christian theology and in religion and the control of violence.

Mark Juergensmeyer is dean of the School of Hawaiian, Asian, and Pacific Studies, University of Hawaii at Monoa, Honolulu, Hawaii. Juergensmeyer has considerable knowledge of religious nationalism and conflict in Asia, with a particularly strong focus on religion and violence.

John Kelsay is a professor in the Department of Religion, Florida State University, Tallahassee, Florida. Kelsay's expertise includes comparative religion with a significant background in Islamic studies.

Samir Khalaf is a visiting professor of sociology at Princeton University, Princeton, New Jersey. Khalaf's studies include Lebanese society and politics, on which he is the author of several books.

Sidney Liskofsky is director of the Jacob Blaustein Institute for the Advancement of Human Rights of the American Jewish Committee, New York. He is a specialist on international organizations and international human rights and is a member of the Executive Committee of the International League for Human Rights.

Ian Lustick is a professor in the Department of Government, Dartmouth College, Hanover, New Hampshire. Lustick is an expert on government, politics, and society in Israel.

Salim Nasr is executive secretary of the Center for Peace and Reconstruction in Lebanon, Washington, D.C. Nasr is a specialist in the religion, society, and politics of Lebanon.

Sulayman Nyang is director of the African Studies Department, Howard University, Washington, D.C. He specializes in the history of Islam in Africa and has particular knowledge of Sudan and Nigeria.

Gerald Powers is an adviser in international affairs to the United States Conference of Catholic Bishops, Washington, D.C. Powers is an expert on religion in Eastern Europe, the ethics of war and peace, and the conflict in Northern Ireland.

Abdulaziz Sachedina is a professor in the Department of Religious Studies, University of Virginia, Charlottesville, Virginia. Sachedina specializes in comparative religion in general, with a particular focus on Islam in the Middle East.

John P. Salzberg is director of the Working Group on the Question of a United Nations Convention on Religious Intolerance, Washington, D.C. He is a specialist in international human rights, with a strong interest in UN consideration of the issue of intolerance based on religion or belief.

H. L. Seneviratne is a professor in the Department of Anthropology, University of Virginia, Charlottesville, Virginia. He is a specialist on religious conflict and intolerance in Sri Lanka.

Elliot Sperling is a professor in the Department of Urali-Ataic Studies, Indiana University, Bloomington, Indiana. Sperling's areas of specialization include Tibetan history, Sino-Tibetan relations, and Buddhism.

Donna Sullivan is with the International League for Human Rights, New York. Sullivan is a legal expert on the UN Declaration against Intolerance.

Stanley Tambiah is a professor in the Department of Anthropology, Harvard University, Cambridge, Massachusetts. Tambiah is an expert on the history, government, politics, and society of Sri Lanka and has considerable general knowledge on the issue of ethnic conflict.

Robert Thurman is a professor in the Department of Religion, Columbia University, New York. He is a specialist on the role of religion in the politics and society of Tibet.

Father Alexander Webster is a senior research associate at the Ethics and Public Policy Center, Washington, D.C. Father Webster is ordained in the Romanian Orthodox church and is a specialist on the church in Eastern Europe and the Soviet Union.

George Weigel is director of the Ethics and Public Policy Center, Washington, D.C. Weigel has considerable expertise in Christian theology, human rights, religion and politics, and religious conflict.